AFTER RUSSIA

After Russia

Poems by
MARINA TSVETAEVA

Translated by
MARY JANE WHITE

BOOKS

Adelaide Books
New York / Lisbon
2020

AFTER RUSSIA
Poems by Marina Tsvetaeva
Translated by Mary Jane White

Cover image: From an original 2013 40 x 30 cm oil on wood painting
of Marina Tsvetaeva by Andrei Nesterov.

Published by Adelaide Books, New York / Lisbon
adelaidebooks.org

Editor-in-Chief
Stevan V. Nikolic

For any information, please address Adelaide Books
at info@adelaidebooks.org

or write to:
Adelaide Books
244 Fifth Ave. Suite D27
New York, NY, 10001

ISBN: 978-1-951896-97-3
Printed in the United States of America

The translations are made under license from Russica Publishers, Inc., 799
Broadway, New York, N. Y., from their five-volume Russian language
edition of Tsvetaeva's poetry and prose, edited and annotated by the
late Alexander Sumerkin.

POEMS OF AN EMIGRANT
AND THREE LONGER POEMS

Poem of the Hill, Poem of the End, New Year's

1922-1927

For

my parents,

Thomas B. and Jane O. White

with much love

and

for my teachers in translation

Mary Barnard, Elena Sokol, John Glad,

Daniel Weissbort

and Alexander Sumerkin

Contents

PRAGUE

A Sibyl

Acknowledgments

POEM OF THE HILL appeared in the Summer 2007 issue of *The New England Review,* ed. C. Dale Young.

POEM OF THE END appeared in the Winter 2009 60th Anniversary Translation Issue of *The Hudson Review,* ed. Paula Deitz and Ron Koury, and was nominated for a Pushcart Prize, and appeared in an English language anthology *From a Terrace in Prague,* ed. Stephan Delbos in Prague (Charles University 2011), where Tsvetaeva wrote it in 1924, and is included in an anthology of translations published over the years by *The Hudson Review, Poets Translate Poets,* (Syracuse 2013).

NEW YEAR'S, An Elegy for Rilke was published by Adastra Press as a letterpress chapbook in an edition of 300 copies in December of 2007, ed. Gary Metras. An earlier version appeared in *Nimrod, International Journal of Poetry and Prose,* ed. Frannie Lindsay.

"To Berlin" appeared in *The Hudson Review,* ed. Paula Deitz.

"Alive, it's not dead . . . ," "Squeezed into this basin of my . . . ," "What, my Muse? Is she still alive . . . ," "Into grey, my temples . . . " appeared in the online journal *Onager Editions,* ed. Sidney Grayling.

"The Dialogue of Hamlet with His Conscience," "The Seafarer," "The Crevasse," "I'll be late to our fixed . . . ," and "Early yet — to no longer be . . . " appeared in the *SIC Online Journal* (Croatia), ed. Tomislav Kuzmanovic.

"So, being still alive, having distributed . . . ," "An Emigrant," and "This is How to Listen Attentively, 1 and 2" appeared in Issue 8 of the online journal, *Taos Journal of International Poetry and Art,* ed. Catherine Strisik and Veronica Golos.

"My Brother," The Hour of the Soul 1, 2 and 3," "As For You, I am Inclined" and "My Spirit" appeared in the July 17, 2016 issue of the online journal, *The Stockholm Review of Literature,* ed. Sofia Capel, Sarvat Hasin, Alex Marsh and Cian McCourt.

"Ophelia — To Hamlet" appeared in 2017 in *Ezra / An Online Journal of Translation,* ed. Peter Thompson.

"Daybreak on the Rails," "No use singing out to her . . . ," and "No, no disputing what's true . . . " appeared in *Vision International,* ed. Bradley R. Strahan.

"Night's whispers: over silk . . . ," "So you will never find me . . . ," and "Lethe's underwater light . . . " appeared in Issue 1 of the online journal, *Peacock Journal,* ed. Bill and Kate Lantry.

"Lethe's underwater light . . . " also appeared in *Peacock Journal Anthology* ed. Bill and Kate Lantry (Little Red Tree 2017).

"Phaedra, A Complaint and An Epistle," and "Eurydice — Orpheus" appeared in *Inventory, No. 7* (Princeton), ed. Kira A. Rose and David Boyd.

"Night Places" and "A Girlfriend" appeared in *Your Impossible Voice,* ed. Keith Powell.

"To 'Helicon,'" as an excerpt to the 1940 cycle addressed to Abram Vishniak appeared in *The Georgia Review,* ed. Stephen Corey, and online in *Poetry Daily* on Monday, January 9, 2017, ed. Don Selby & Diane Boller.

"An Attempt at Jealousy" appeared in *Exchanges*, the online journal of the University of Iowa's MFA Program in Literary Translation, ed. Patricia Hartman, and in the April 2017 issue of *The Odessa Review* (Ukraine), ed. Valdislav Davidzon.

An earlier version of the essay TRANSLATOR'S INTRODUCTION: WRITING TSVETAEVA INTO OUR AMERICAN CANON appeared in *Exchanges*, the online journal of the University of Iowa's MFA Program in Literary Translation, ed. Patricia Hartman, and a shorter version of the same essay appeared in the April 2017 issue of *The Odessa Review* (Ukraine), ed. Vladislav Davidzon.

"Clouds, 1, 2 and 3" appeared in *Mayday Magazine,* ed. Okla Elliott.

"A Window," "To Honor Time," "His Sister," "Night," and "To Steal . . . " appeared in *Numero Cinq,* an online journal, ed. Douglas Glover and Benjamin Woodward.

"To Steal . . . " appeared in the anthology *The Music of Time: Poetry in the 20th Century* by John Burnside (Profile Books, Ltd. UK, 2019, 2020).

"Poets, 1, 2 and 3" appeared in *OmniVerse*, ed. Rusty Morrison and Gillian Hamel.

"Time I get the message . . . ," "Fierce valley . . . ," and "Through all the tedious tasks of the day . . . " appeared in the March 21, 2017 issue of *Off course*, an online journal, ed. by Ricardo and Isabel Nirenberg at the University of Albany.

"The Consecration," "Having haggled for a stirrup," "Dis—tance, versts, miles . . . ," "I bow, with my regards, to the Russian rye . . . ," appeared in *Reunion: The Dallas Review*, A University of Texas at Dallas Publication of the School of Arts and Humanities, ed. Chelsea Barnard.

"Trees," "Having lost faith in mortals . . . ," "When down a string of insults — my incensed . . . ," "Like bathers, in a loose circle . . . ," "Friends! My gathered brothers . . . ," "Deserters? — Adjuncts? . . . ," "With neither paint, nor brush . . . ," "She who slept untroubled by visions . . . ," "Someone rides — to mortal victory . . . ," "What intuitions . . . " appeared in the Summer 2017 issue of *Adelaide Magazine* (print and online in English in NYC and Lisbon), ed. Stevan V. Nikolic.

"Trees," "Having lost faith in mortals . . . ," "When down a string of insults — my incensed . . . ," "Like bathers, in a loose circle . . . ," "Friends! My gathered brothers . . . ," "Deserters? — Adjuncts? . . . ," "With neither paint, nor brush . . . ," "She who slept untroubled by visions . . . ," "Someone rides — to mortal victory . . . ," "What intuitions . . . " also appeared in *Inventory* #8 (Princeton), ed. David Boyd.

"Lines 8, 9 and 10" appeared in the October 2017 issue of *Waxwing* (online), ed. Curtis Bauer.

"Poem of the Gates" appeared in the Winter 2017 issue of *Witness Magazine*, University of Nevada, Las Vegas, ed. Oscar Oswald.

"The insinuations of your hair . . . ," "Scythians 1, 2 and 3," and "A Letter" appeared in *The Peacock Journal*, ed. Bill and Kate Lantry.

"About Factories," "God 1, 2 and 3," "By Correspondence" appeared in the December 2017 issue of *[SIC] Online Journal*, ed. Tomislav Kuzmanovic.

"Lines 1-10" appeared in the June 2018 issue of *[SIC] Online Journal*, ed. Tomislav Kuzmanovic.

"For some — there are no laws . . . ," "To Berlin" (reprinted from *The Hudson Review*), "You'll see for yourself — in time! . . . ," and "A light-silvery mold . . . " appeared in *Cardinal Points* in 2019, ed. Boris Dralyuk.

"Achilles on the Wall," "The Last Sailor," "The Cry of Stations," "The Prague Knight" and "Life Train" appeared in the December 21, 2017 issue of *Off course*, an online journal, ed. by Ricardo and Isabel Nirenberg at the University of Albany.

"The Two of Us, 1, 2 and 3," "An Island," Under a Shawl," "All by herself—Helen gazes over the rooftops . . . ," "I sang like arrows and eels . . . ," and "A blizzard sweeps the floors . . . " appeared in *Anomaly #27,* ed. Anna Rosenwong.

"A Sibyl, 1, 2 and 3," and "Brooks, 1 and 2" appeared in *Meluzina,* an online journal of the Prague Summer Program for Writers, ed. Ema Katrovas.

"A Letter" and "A Lullaby" appeared in *Cutthroat 24,* ed. William Pitt Root and Pam Uschuk.

"God help us, the smoke . . . ," appeared in *About Place Journal: Poetry: Dignity as an Endangered Species in the 21st Century,* ed. Pamela Uschuk, CMarie Fuhrman and Maggie Miller.

"Ariadne, 1 and 2" and "Words and Meanings 1, 2 and 3" appeared in the online journal, *Taos Journal of International Poetry and Art,* ed. Catherine Strisik and Veronica Golos.

"Find yourself more credulous lovers . . . ," "Remember this stricture: Earth is . . . ," "When, if ever dear God . . . ," "A tree's – first – quiver . . . ," "The sunburned one has—his axe and plow . . . ," and "Morning! As neither arrow, nor stone . . . " appeared in *FOUR CENTURIES Russian Poetry in Translation,* ed. Ilya Perelmuter.

"A Ravine 1 and 2," "An ancient vanity runs in my veins . . . ", "Escape," "I wander—not one to build a home . . . ," "I love—but the pain lives on . . . " appeared in *Inventory Journal #10,* ed. Daniel Dominguez and Apolline Pernet.

My thanks to the National Endowment for the Arts for a poetry fellowship in 1979 and a later translation fellowship in 1985 which supported this work.

Preface

MARINA TSVETAEVA (1892-1941)
A BIOGRAPHICAL SKETCH

"To write poetry is already to translate, from the mother tongue into another — whether into French or German is of no moment. No language is the mother tongue. To write poetry is to translate."

Tsvetaeva's letter to Rilke of 6 July 1926.

Marina Tsvetaeva was born in Moscow in 1892, and began to publish in her teens, to multiple good reviews by Russian literary critics.

She was a working contemporary of Anna Akhmatova, Osip Mandelstam, Boris Pasternak and Rainer Maria Rilke, all of whom were important to her as rival, lover, correspondent and mentor, respectively.

BERLIN

Tsvetaeva left the Soviet Union in 1922 to reunite with her husband, Sergei Efron, after a four year wartime separation during the Russian Revolution. Efron had already been evacuated to the West through Turkey into Czechoslovakia with remnants of the defeated White Army.

"Marina Tsvetaeva stepped off the Riga-Berlin train at the Berlin-Charlottenburg station on May 15, 1922. She went there, rather than to Prague where her husband lived, because she had more books to publish and Berlin was at that time the publishing capital for Russian literature. . . . the population of Russians in Berlin in 1922 numbered 100,000 . . . . there was a great hunger for new Russian books and periodicals. A large number of publishing houses arose in Berlin in response to this demand."[1]

"From the moment she arrived in Berlin, Tsvetaeva emerged as a major literary celebrity. Editors of journals sought her contributions. She was lionized by publishers and fellow writers . . . . she observed and participated in what she later called 'a general exchange of fees and manuscripts.' With her literary earnings, she could afford to stay at a decent hotel and to buy, for the first time in years, some good new clothes for herself and her daughter."[2]

Tsvetaeva and Efron's anticipated reunion did not preclude her affair with the publisher of two of her earlier collections, Abram G. Vishniak (1895-1943) [Helicon], about and to whom the great majority of her poems in 1922 in Berlin were written.

---

[1] Simon Karlinsky, *Marina Tsvetaeva, The Woman, her World and her Poetry* (Cambridge: Cambridge University Press, 1985), 114-115.

[2] Ibid., 116.

"He was twenty-seven years old and happily married to a lovely young woman with whom he had a four-year-old son. He had published Tsvetaeva's *Separation* and was planning to publish *Craft*. Tsvetaeva impressed Vishniak both as a poet and as a woman. Her precocious, not-quite ten-year-old daughter noted in her diary:

'Marina talks to Helicon like a Titan, and she is as incomprehensible to him as the North Pole is to an inhabitant of the Near East and just as enticing, [. . .] I saw that he turns toward her like a plant to the sun, with the whole of his rumpled stem. But the sun is distant because Marina's essence is reticence and clenched teeth, while he is pliant and soft like a pea sprout.'

. . . . Tsvetaeva mistook his admiration and his professional interest in her work for something more personal and intimate. . . . [Tsvetaeva's feelings for Vishniak] which are a curious mix of passion, condescension and maternal concern . . . were . . . reflected in a group of poems dated June and July 1922 . . . .[but] Tsvetaeva's one-sided infatuation with Abram Vishniak lasted only a few weeks. When it was over, she thought of him with revulsion."[3]

Tsvetaeva's brief period in Berlin, lasting until July 31 of 1922, was a very productive period. She wrote a total of 22 poems, with poems arriving every other day or so, or sometimes two poems a day.

[3] Ibid., 117-119.

PRAGUE

Two photographs from the time Tsvetaeva lived in Prague where she wrote most of her final collection of short lyrics, *After Russia* (Paris, 1928).

Above: Tsvetaeva and her daughter Alya.

Below: Tsvetaeva front left, her husband Sergei Efron, back left, and Konstantin Rodzevich, front right, about whom Tsvetaeva wrote "Poem of the Hill" and "Poem of the End."

The pace of writing short lyrics, at one or two a day or every other day continued as Tsvetaeva moved to Prague in August of 1922, and did not begin to decline until about 1925. It was interrupted by other work: essays and letters, but most dramatically by the longer *poemas* "Poem of the Hill" and "Poem of the End," both written about the end of her affair with Konstantin Rodzevich, and included here in this present collection of translations, inserted chronologically among her shorter lyrics.

So, who was this Konstantin Rodzevich, Tsvetaeva's *grand amour*?

"In the Soviet Union, Tsvetaeva's editor and annotator Anna Saakiants as well as [Tsvetaeva's daughter] Ariadna Efron in her memoirs have applied to Rodzevich such adjectives as 'knightly,' 'chivalrous' and 'gallant.' Tsvetaeva's daughter told her readers that the man her mother fell in love with was a Communist and a hero of the Spanish Civil War and the French Resistance during World War II. She was, of course, referring to his situation and beliefs in the late 1930s, many years after he and Tsvetaeva had parted ways. Rodzevich's membership in the French Communist Party and activities in Spain are brought up to create a heroic halo for him and to exculpate Tsvetaeva retroactively of loving an exiled White officer back in 1923 and of having committed adultery, which is usually an unmentionable subject in Soviet literary studies of admired writers.

"The testimony of persons who knew Rodzevich at the time of his relationship with Tsvetaeva is far less flattering. Sergei Efron, in a letter [to Russian critic and family-friend] Max Voloshin, called Rodzevich 'a small-time Casanova.' Nikolai Elenev, who knew Rodzevich well in Prague, described him in his memoir on Tsvetaeva as 'sly and congenitally false.' And the woman whom Rodzevich married some time after the end of his relationship with Tsvetaeva told Veronique Lossky he was 'a total nonentity' and 'a seductive swine' (she and Rodzevich were divorced shortly after their marriage). Tsvetaeva, it would seem also at first took a negative view of Konstantin Rodzevich, greeting him with mockery and finding that she had nothing in common with him. Then, after the departure of Sergei for [a] tuberculosis sanatorium [and the placement of their daughter in boarding school], [the] affair began. Its doomed, hopeless quality is conveyed in the poem ['Night Places'] ('Nochnye mesta'), dated October 4, 1923 . . . ,"[4] included in this collection.

"Tsvetaeva's affair with Rodzevich lasted from September to December 1923. She devoted the month of January 1924 to writing 'Poem of the Hill,' the first of her two poetic epitaphs to that relationship. The second and much longer epitaph, 'Poem of the End,' took from February to June"[5] [of 1924].

"'Poem of the Hill' is a poem of great pain. Its indiscriminately vengeful tone and the destructive urge of its final sections are sure to repel many readers. Tsvetaeva herself may not have been entirely satisfied by such a bitter memorial to her love, because immediately after completing this poem she embarked on its companion piece, 'Poem of the End.' This poem is genuinely narrative and highly dramatic. It describes

[4] Ibid., 136-137.

[5] Ibid., 138.

in great detail the evening on which the lovers decide
that their relationship must end. The reader follows
them on their strolls through the streets and suburbs
of Prague, a walk by the river, a visit to a café and
their conversations during which the need to separate
is articulated. In the last two sections, the man is unable to hold back his tears, making the woman realize
he loves and needs her and causing some merriment
on the part of three prostitutes who happen to witness the final farewell. Every word, glance and action
of her departing lover is analyzed by the desperate
woman, with a constant conflict between her imagination and what her reason and senses tell her to be
facts. The method is that of a stream of conscious-
ness, conveyed in a choppy, telegraphic diction, with
insight and expressivity that make 'Poem of the End'
one of the great psychological poems in the Russian
language.'[6]

As an emigrant — in the daily world of the mundane —
Tsvetaeva struggled with the demands of life in the small villages
surrounding Prague where for the most part and for most of
her time in Czechoslovakia she found herself to have washed up
into considerable poverty with her young daughter and depen-
dent-student-war-veteran husband, with the addition in 1925 of
an infant son. The family was supported by Tsvetaeva's writing,
small refugee pensions to herself and her husband from the Czech
government, supplemented by direct gifts from Czech literary
friends like Anna Teskova, and various older women friends

[6] Ibid., 141.

"There was only one head of state in the whole of the Western world, it seems, who realized just what had happened in Russia, what was involved and what it meant for the rest of the world. That was Tomas Garrigue Masaryk, the first president of Czechoslovakia, which had regained its independence in the aftermath of World War I. He had frequently visited Russia and happened to be there during both the February regime and the October Revolution. Through his knowledge of Russian language and culture, Masaryk had acquired a clearer picture of Russian social and political realities than most foreigners. He understood that the triumph of Bolshevism did not spell a victory for democracy and that the people fleeing from Russia were, for the most part, not tsarist reactionaries. His partly American background (his wife was an American and he had lived in America and taught at American universities) had instilled in Masaryk a healthily pluralist outlook. While Masaryk's personal sympathies were undoubtedly with the more democratic Russian circles, his government welcomed refugees of every ilk. At the university which the Czech government had organized in Prague for exiled Russians, former officers of the monarchist White armies, such as Sergei Efron, found themselves in the same classes with those who had served in anarchist or S[ocial] R[evoluntionary] counter-revolutionary units and who during the civil war had disliked the Whites almost as much as they hated the Bolsheviks."[7]

---

[7] Ibid., 125.

"The winter of 1924-5 was spent by Tsvetaeva in near-seclusion in the village of Vsenory. Her son was born there on February 1, 1925. As recalled in the memoirs of [her daughter] Ariana Efron, Tsvetaeva was attended at the time of delivery by six loyal women friends, among them Anna Andreyeva, Maria ('Mouna') Bulgakova (the daughter of the noted theologian, she later married Konstantin Rodzevich) and Alexandra Turzhansky. A few days later Tsvetaeva was visited by her Czech friend, Anna Teskova. 'Grey-haired, majestic, inwardly regal,' was how Tsvetaeva described Teskova after that visit. 'An aquiline nose, like a mountain crest between the sky-blue lakes of her genuinely calm eyes, her grey hair arranged in a crown. A high neck, a high bosom — everything about her is high.' Teskova was a journalist, a translator of Russian writers and the president of the cultural section of the Prague Czech-Russian Society, where she had occasionally invited Tsvetaeva to give readings of her poetry and prose. In later years she was to prove a loyal friend who unfailingly came to Tsvetaeva's help with prolonging the Czech stipend and in other financial and administrative matters. Tsvetaeva dedicated her verse cycle 'Trees' ('Derev'ia') [included in this collection] to Anna Teskova; their correspondence, which continued until Tsvetaeva's return to the Soviet Union, is an important biographical and literary source."[8]

During this time, Tsvetaeva continued to publish prolifically in the periodical press, and as Karlinsky reports, to be noticed there:

[8] Ibid., 139.

"Lev Mnukhin's bibliographical guide to publications about Tsvetaeva's life and activities (it excludes publications of her own writings) registers between one and twelve items per year during [her early Russian] period 1910-21. For 1922, the figure jumps to forty-seven. For the next five years there are between forty and sixty items per year (reviews of Tsvetaeva's work, discussions of it or news items about her) to be found in the Soviet and the Russian émigré press. Russian publications abroad treated her for the most part as a famous and admired poet, though we find some censorious items occasioned by the unconventionality of her style. But in the Soviet Union, where Tsvetaeva's work went on appearing in anthologies and literary miscellanies and her books were on sale until about 1926, the more prominent critical voices were invariably hostile. The hostility was prompted less by the fact of Tsvetaeva's emigration (poets who remained in Russia, such as Akhmatova, were often treated even worse in the Soviet press) than by undisguised misogyny."[9]

Ugly misogynist reviews issued from Mandelstam (sadly), Leon Trotsky (predictably), Semion Rodov, Vladimir Mayakovsky, (possibly as instigated by Lenin's wife, Nadezhda Krupskaya, with Lenin's full approval), while she was in Prague.

Summing up the time during which this collection was written, and Tsvetaeva's time in Prague, Karlinsky has offered this assessment:

[9] Ibid., 128.

"It has been said that Tsvetaeva came to idealize Czechoslovakia, that she longed for it only after she had left it and that she cared little for it when she lived there. But it is quite understandable why her Czech period looked so attractive to her in retrospect. Despite emotional turmoil and occasional physical discomfort, she was better off personally and professionally during that time than she would ever be again. Her books were published and they found appreciative audiences both in the Soviet Union and abroad. She earned money with her writings and did not experience the kind of indigence that she lived with during the time of War Communism in Moscow and would know again a decade later in Paris. The years 1922-5 were for Marina Tsvetaeva a time of achievement and hope and, as we can now see, one of the happiest periods of her life."[10]

"The poems of *After Russia* are rich and rewarding when read on their own, without commentary. But the publication of Tsvetaeva's correspondence in recent years has revealed the hidden themes and addressees of this volume. Much of the book is about the four men to whom she was drawn during the years when these poems were written and about the impossibility of a desired, lasting union with any of them. The main protagonist of *After Russia* (how much better the original title *Secret Intentions* would have described this aspect of the book!) is Boris Pasternak, by virtue of both the sheer number of poems addressed to him and the intensity of the emotions he aroused in the poet. His three supporting

[10] Ibid., 147.

players are Abram Vishniak, Alexander Bakhrakh and Konstantin Rodzevich, who all proved in one way or another unworthy of the expectations vested in them, but who inspired magnificent poems during their span in Tsvetaeva's orbit."[11]

By spring of 1925, Tsvetaeva moved on to Paris, where, in 1928, her Berlin and Prague poems were collected into her final published book of shorter lyrics, *After Russia*.

> "By 1925, Russian literature of the twentieth century had divided into its two, distinct, somewhat artificial branches, Soviet and émigré. The center for émigré literature was now Paris, and that was where most of the working Russian writers abroad were headed."[12]

In part, as a result of these divisions, literary disputes and her husband's political allegiances in Paris, "[t]he book that by rights should have secured [Tsvetaeva] her greatest triumph sank with very few ripples" beyond the unreserved praise of émigré commentator (and the addressee of "An Attempt at Jealousy"), Mark Slonim.

Russian critic Simon Karlinsky, also her biographer, offers this judgment of her work of this period:

> "If we were to select the verse collection by Tsvetaeva in which her poetic craft reaches its highest peak, and her human and poetic stature its more awesome

[11] Ibid., 187.

[12] Ibid., 150.

dimension and sweep, we would have to choose *Posle Rossii [After Russia].*"[13]

"The shorter lyric poems which Tsvetaeva wrote in Berlin and Czechoslovakia between 1922 and 1925 are among her most profound and best-structured."[14]

"*After Russia* is a book in which Tsvetaeva found a new way of looking at life and art, evolved a successful personal idiom in which to express this view, and did so in a poetry of unique metrical freshness and verbal beauty."[15]

The collection *After Russia* includes poems in Tsvetaeva's quietest voice, such as "So, being alive, having distributed . . . " and "To Steal . . . "

There are poems written in her most brilliant and cutting invective, such as "An Emigrant" and "Thank God for the Rich."

There are poems of exile, "Daybreak on the Rails," of lamentation over the separation from her Russian readership, and friends, principally Boris Pasternak, in the sequences "Lines," and "The Two of Us," and in the two concluding poems of *After Russia*, "Dis—tance, versts, miles . . . ," and "I bow, with my regards, to the Russian rye . . . ."

There are poems expressing both pique, "Life Train," and empathy for her new Czech neighbors, "God help us, the smoke . . . " and "A Passage," for factory-workers, "About Factories," and "Poem of the Gates," for seamstresses, and for Jews in "Poem of the End."

---

[13] Simon Karlinsky, *Marina Cvetaeva: Her Life and Art* (Berkeley: University of California Press, 1966), 193-94.

[14] Simon Karlinsky, *Marina Tsvetaeva: The Woman, her World and her Poetry* (Cambridge: Cambridge University Press, 1985), 184.

[15] Ibid., 188.

There's even a hilarious look-back political tour-de-force brimming with double-entendre about the Soviet Red Guards, "The Floor Polishers' Song."

God is generally a frustrating absence, as in "God." But figures from the Bible repeatedly appear in "My Lute," "The Lesson of Thomas," and "Magdalene," as do various Greeks and their gods in "A Sibyl," "Phaedra," "Eurydice to Orpheus," "Ariadne," "Achilles on the Wall" and "All by herself—Helen gazes over the rooftops . . . ."

There are poems expressing considerable open frustration with her marriage to Sergei Efron, "But it's cramped for two . . . ," and with any marriage, "The Consecration."

There are incantations, such as "Scythians," lullabies, and a remarkable poem that might as well been written for her son, Georgy (Mur) born in 1925, "A Sibyl — To Her Newborn."

There are poems about poetic practice, and her anticipation of entry, or not, into the canon, such as "Poets."

There are remarkable love poems, and poems of near-cavalier dismissal of several identified lovers, for example, "An Attempt at Jealousy," written to critic and friend, Mark Slonim.

Many of the poems engage in identified dialog with Boris Pasternak, including this poem of barely-restrained frustration:

Patiently, as one pounds stone,
Patiently, as one waits to die,
Patiently, as one absorbs news,
Patiently, as one nurses revenge —

I wait for you (fingers laced —
As a consort waits on a Sovereign)
Patiently, as one waits on rhyme,
Patiently, as one worries a cuticle.

I wait for you (eyes — downcast,
Teeth in my lips. Stunned. A paving brick).
Patiently, as one holds off coming,
Patiently, as one strings beads.

Creak of a sledge, answering creak
Of a door: roar of the taiga's winds.
The imperial decree is issued:
— Regime change, entry of a new grandee.

Welcome, then:
Unearthly home that it is —
It *is* my own.

In her unrequited relationships of letters — with Pasternak in 1922-1925, with the young critic Alexander Bakhrakh in early 1923, and with Rilke in 1926 — as in many of her emotional relationships in the flesh — as with Vishniak in Berlin in 1922, or Konstantin Rodzevich in Prague in late 1923, or otherwise — Tsvetaeva was supremely and powerfully possessive, controlling the "role" of her partner in her imagination, frequently calling on myth and incantation to write the script.

As Tess Gallagher describes her, Tsvetaeva "is always a woman loving like a woman — heedless and remorselessly, full of savoring and overreach, but haughty too and in the plenitude of her beauty, both physical and spiritual."[16]

This particular collection of translations is meant to allow readers of English to be able to explore the relationship of

---

[16] "Translating the fine excess of spirit in Marina Tsvetaeva," Michael M. Naydan and Slava L. Yastremski, *Marina Tsvetaeva, The Essential Poetry* (London: Glagoslav, 2015), 12.

Tsvetaeva's near-daily practice of writing the shorter lyrics of *After Russia* to establishing her capacity to respond with the very fine longer *poemas* to the emotionally-charged 1923 affair with Konstantin Rodzevich that occasioned her writing both "Poem of the Hill" and "Poem of the End," and to the equally emotionally-charged 1926 correspondence with Rilke from which she harvested as she wrote "New Year's," her early 1927 elegy for him.

"In March 1926, Pasternak happened to see a privately-circulated, typewritten copy of 'Poem of the End' in Moscow. Unappreciated and perhaps not even understood by its protagonist, Konstantin Rodzevich, the poem ricocheted to Pasternak, causing an emotional explosion. In her earlier cycles of poems addressed to him, such as 'Telegraph Wires' ["Lines" in this collection] 1923, and 'The Two' ('Dvoe') ["The Two of Us" in this collection] 1924, Tsvetaeva wrote of Pasternak as her ideal soul-mate, the only person in the world who was fully attuned to her wavelength. Now, in the wake of reading 'Poem of the End,' there came a torrent of letters from Pasternak, in which he offered himself to Tsvetaeva as her ideal reader, ideal critic and as a man desperately in love: 'You were sent to me straight from Heaven, you fit the ultimate extremes of my soul. You are mine, you were always mine and my whole life is for you.' And later: 'What a huge, devilishly huge artist you are, Marina!' By April 20, Pasternak's passionate outpourings culminated in an offer either to abandon his wife and child at once and come to join Tsvetaeva or to postpone this for one year: 'There is nothing else left to be said. I have a goal in life and this goal is you.' Tsvetaeva recommended postponement. As she was to write to Anna Teskova five years later: 'In the summer of 1926, after reading somewhere my 'Poem of the End,' Boris conceived a mad yearning for me and wanted to come, but I declined. I did not want a catastrophe for *everyone*.' On May 8 Pasternak wrote that he accepted her decision: 'You have indicated the boundaries.'"[17]

However, during this time of emotional turmoil, Pasternak did Tsvetaeva a generous personal, professional and poetic service, one which ultimately led to Tsvetaeva's writing what is, perhaps, her finest *poema*, the concluding piece in this collection, "New Year's," her elegy for Rilke:

"On April 12, 1926 Boris Pasternak wrote a letter of introduction for Marina Tsvetaeva to Rainer Maria Rilke, providing Rilke with Tsvetaeva's address in the Parisian suburb of Bellevue where she was then living in exile. Rilke responded on May 3 with a first letter to Tsvetaeva, covering autographed copies of his 'Duino Elegies' and 'Sonnets to Orpheus.'

"Throughout that summer the three poets wrote to each other. In his fourth letter to Tsvetaeva, June 8, Rilke enclosed a poem he wrote that day for her, 'Elegie.'[18]

"When Rilke died of leukemia on December 29, 1926, Tsvetaeva learned of his death from Mark

---

[17] Karlinsky, *Marina Tsvetaeva, The Woman, her World and her Poetry*, (Cambridge: Cambridge University Press, 1985), 161.

[18] A very fine English *en-face* translation of Rilke's poem to Tsvetaeva by Stephen Mitchell appears in his *The Selected Poetry of Rainer Maria Rilke* (New York: Vintage International), 288-291.

Slonim, who asked her to write a piece for the Russian émigré press. Instead, she wrote this elegy, 'New Year's,' drawing heavily upon both the correspondence of that summer and Rilke's poem for her.

"In his extensive essay on 'New Year's,' Joseph Brodsky judges Tsvetaeva's elegy to be 'in many respects a landmark not only in her own work but in Russian poetry as a whole.' (*Less Than One*)."[19]

In 1939, Tsvetaeva and her son chose to follow her husband and daughter back to the Soviet Union, "like a dog," as she noted in the margin of a manuscript left behind her. Back in the USSR, Sergei Efron, was arrested and executed by the KGB; her daughter, Ariadna (Alya), was also arrested and committed to a labor camp where she lost an unborn child; her teen-aged son, Georgy (Mur) found himself unsettled and unhappy in the USSR, and later died as a soldier in World War II — his death coming not so long after Tsvetaeva hanged herself on August 31, 1941, in Elabuga, where she and her son had been evacuated south from wartime Moscow.

At the time of her death, she was 48.

---

[19] "Translator's Introduction," Mary Jane White, *New Year's, an elegy for Rilke* (Easthampton, MA: Adastra Press, 2007).

Translator's Introduction: Writing Tsvetaeva Into Our American Canon

By Mary Jane White

As I reflect upon my relationship as a reader-translator of Tsvetaeva, I find that as a American woman who began reading, writing and translating poetry in the early 1970s, I share a generational point of view with my near-contemporary Tess Gallagher as expressed in her introductory essay "Translating the fine excess of spirit in Marina Tsvetaeva":[20]

> "Marina Tsvetaeva holds a very special place in my memory of the search for women writers who might offer examples of what to admire and to which we might aspire."

---

[20] "Translating the fine excess of spirit in Marina Tsvetaeva," Naydan, op. cit., 9-13.

"The early 1970s female models for young women poets like myself, as we began to form our poetic voices, were either hermetic such as Emily Dickinson — who was shuttered away, with her bounty hidden in mason jars because her genius had been thwarted by male publishing predilections — or at the other end of the scale, the explosive cauldron of pent up righteous anger and truth-telling of Sylvia Plath and Anne Sexton — for which one was grateful, while feeling guiltily that one had perhaps been ritually saved by their suicides from similar psychic trauma."

My own first early 1970s introduction to Marina Tsvetaeva came as I was beginning to read and struggling to write poetry in English, while also beginning and struggling to learn the rudiments of inflected Russian grammar at Reed College. Tsvetaeva was introduced by a brief selection of *en-face* translations in an anthology edited by Vladimir Markov and Merrill Sparks, *Modern Russian Poetry*,[21] one of a number of textbooks for a Russian literature course taught by Elena Sokol.

I remember the particular Tsvetaeva poem that struck me as memorable was "An Attempt at Jealousy." Where I had ever heard a voice like that? Never!

Here was, as Tess Gallagher describes her, "the Tsvetaeva who really wants to love like the gods, not like a mere human being" . . . for whom "it was not easy to find lovers who could soar with her,[22] the Tsvetaeva who "uses her poetry to regain her

---

[21] Vladimir Markov and Merrill Sparks, *Modern Russian Poetry, An Anthology With Verse Translations* (New York: The Bobbs-Merrill Company, Inc., 1966), 429-449.

[22] "Translating the fine excess of spirit in Marina Tsvetaeva," Naydan, op. cit., 11.

emotional balance. Instead of cutting a lover off for leaving her, or becoming the victim, she turns the tables on them and lets them feel what *they* have lost in abandoning *their* love of her. This was a newly articulated paradigm for women poets all over the world trying to do more than lick wounds in the stance of a victim."[23]

Later, in the mid-1970s, as I was writing toward my MFA in Poetry from the Iowa Writers' Workshop, and finishing a law degree, I had the opportunity to work a couple of seasons for the International Writing Program as an assistant to Directors Paul and Hualing Engle; each week I was handed literal "trots" from various world languages to translate writers' presentations (on deadline!) into English.

During those rich and busy years at Iowa, I also studied with Russian translators, John Glad and Daniel Weissbort (who with Ted Hughes founded and edited *Modern Poetry in Translation*), and was able to contribute my own first translations of Russian poems by Nikolay Gumilyov, Vladislav Khodasevich, Vyacheslav Ivanov and Edward Limonov to the anthology they co-edited, *Russian Poetry: The Modern Period,* (1978, University of Iowa Press), a New York Times Notable Book of the Year.

Then, in February of 1978, I turned my attention to translating Tsvetaeva because:

" . . . as an anonymous member of an Iowa City audience I had the opportunity to ask Russian-born poet Joseph Brodsky several questions about Anna Akhmatova — whose reputation remains wider than Tsvetaeva's. Akhmatova and Brodsky were acquainted in Moscow when she was a very old woman and he a young man. He confessed that they had gossiped, as poets will do, about other poets,

[23] Ibid.

but that Akhmatova then 'was awfully humble. She used to say that 'in comparison with [Pushkin] and Tsvetaeva I am just a little cow. I am a cow,' that's what she used to say.'[24] I think now of what Tsvetaeva might have given to have been eavesdropping then![25]

Or later, as Brodsky gave his 1978 recommendation for reading:

"Well, if you are talking about the twentieth century, I'll give you a list of poets. Akhmatova, Mandelstam, Tsvetaeva (and she is the greatest one, in my view. The greatest poet in the twentieth century was a woman).[26]

This exchange is in curious accord with Tess Gallagher's own recent comparative description of the differing appeals of Akhmatova and Tsvetaeva:

"In placing Tsvetaeva's appeal to American contemporary poetry of the present and myself in the 1970s, I believe she has been the more dangerous and unwieldy model when compared to Akhmatova, who became so important to us as a sign of stature under political and emotional duress, attracting translators such as Jane Kenyon whose own work was greatly emboldened by Akhmatova."[27]

---

[24] *The Iowa Review* 9 (4): 4-5.

[25] Ibid.

[26] Ibid.

[27] "Translating the fine excess of spirit in Marina Tsvetaeva," Naydan, op. cit., 11.

Brodsky's direct answers to my questions-from-the-floor raised in me an early ambition to write a Tsvetaeva in English that would serve my own and the next generation of American poets, a translation that would let Tsvetaeva "wear fully the stature of the English she might have given us, had she written in English."[28]

Since 1978, I've continued to work on reading and translating Tsvetaeva, taking Brodsky's response as a sort of assignment, for nearly forty years. There was one long unsteady break of 15 years between 1991- 2006 I took to raise my son out of his childhood autism. What an emotional day it was in the late fall of 2005 when my son's recovery from autism seemed secure, when I brought my large poetry library, my little red notebooks, and my dictionaries up from the basement where I had banished them into tightly-taped boxes, so they would not present any competing temptation to the attention my son's recovery and special education had required.

The hospitable Benedictine monks of St. John's University, Collegeville, Minnesota, who provided my son's rigorously academic high school education, kindly opened their monastery there to me each weekend, giving me a vacant monk's cell . . . a place to begin to read, to write and to translate again.

On weekdays and court days I resumed dragging my thrice-re-bound *Oxford Russian-English Dictionary* and little red moleskin notebooks from courthouse to courthouse throughout five counties of Northeast Iowa, working in fits and starts while waiting for my assigned legal hearings and cases to be called — trial law being like war: hurry up, and wait. What you do during the wait is another life . . .

Publication of the translations of the three longer *poemas* included in this collection followed quickly in 2006, 2007, and 2009 in *The New England Review*, (ed. C. Dale Young), *The*

[28] Ibid., 13.

Hudson Review (ed. Paula Deitz), and in chapbook publication by Adastra Press (ed. Gary Metras).

The translation of "Poem of the End" first appeared in *The Hudson Review's 60th Anniversary Edition*, (nominated for a Pushcart Prize), and was then included in *The Hudson Review's* recently-published anthology drawing upon sixty years of their translation publications, *Poets Translate Poets,* (Syracuse: 2013) in most-distinguished company — of poets, and translators alike.

Then Stephan Delbos, editor of . . . *B O D Y* online magazine, who lives and works in Prague, called me one day out of the blue to ask if I was "the Mary Jane White who translates Tsvetaeva" and his call eventually led to *The Hudson Review* allowing Delbos to include my translation of "Poem of the End" in his anthology, *From A Terrace in Prague, A Prague Poetry Anthology,* (Univerzita Karlova v Praze: 2011), and to my travelling to Prague to give a reading of "Poem of the End," sponsored by . . . *B O D Y* and by the small and lovely Tsvetaeva Centre there, now located in Vsenory.

Prague, in winter, was just as I imagined — well, you bring your own eyes and expectations to any travel experience — but I was able to walk the neighborhoods and bridges of Prague, and spend a day in Tsvetaeva's favorite Café Slavia at the foot of the Charles Bridge talking to Russian-born students, and listening to Tsvetaeva being read to me in Russian.

What a great privilege is has been to *try* to translate Tsvetaeva! Beginning with her early cycles, "Miles I and II,"[29]

"[m]y approach to translating Tsvetaeva has been to produce an accurate literal version that is not painful

---

[29] Mary Jane White, *Starry Sky to Starry Sky, Poems by Mary Jane White with Translations of Marina Tsvetaeva* (Stevens Point, Wisconsin: Holy Cow! Press, 1988), 49-92.

or awkward for an American speaker to read. Early in the process, I looked up each word in the *Oxford Russian-English Dictionary* and noted each meaning of the word and every idiom in which it is reported to be used. This part of translating has the same attraction for me as crossword puzzles do for other people; it's like knitting, or doing tax returns. It produces the calm high of word or number intoxication. My purpose in doing this is to obtain, by osmosis, a sure feeling for the texture of the particular language Tsvetaeva chose, the texture, if you will, of her diction. This slow acquaintance and the notes—to which I refer back—aid me in making a sure choice among the various meanings for each individual word."

"I make an effort to keep the material of a single line confined to a single line of translation — this, to preserve the *pace* of the original as much as possible. This is not an original idea at all. While a student at Reed College in Portland, Oregon, I traveled often to Vancouver, Washington to visit Mary Barnard, the wonderful translator of Sappho. It was she who convinced me of the value of this general rule of fidelity and pointed out to me how preserving the pace of the original is useful in reproducing its tone. Think of how speeding up or slowing down a film may introduce an overall comic or lyrical effect. In the interest of maintaining this fidelity to pace and tone I try never to omit, or pad. Tsvetaeva can be very abbreviated and abrupt in her original. She would suffer from 'explanation added.'"

"I do not attempt to translate in rhyme or meter, although Tsvetaeva's poems are rhymed and metered with the same fresh and surprising closeness of, say, Ezra Pound in *Hugh Selwyn Mauberley.* It has been observed that rhyming at least is much easier to do in Russian than in English. In part, this is due to the fact that Russian is an inflected language. This inflection also results in a greater variety and syllable depth of rhyme and of assonance than in English—a rhyme might extend through as many as three syllables, and an assonance might be found upon a stressed vowel or vowel sound three syllables deep into the rhyming words. So, as you read, you must think of all this as missing."[30]

Here is how Tsvetaeva's Russian critic Karlinsky describes what-remains-missing from these translations:

"Already in 1922, Andrei Bely, in his brief review of Tsvetaeva's [earlier] collection *Separation,* pointed out the central importance of the choriamb for the haunting effect of her metrical patterns: 'The [impulse forward] is astounding in the plasticity of its gestures . . . . ; and the choriamb (– UU –), which Tsvetaeva wields magnificently, is the obedient expression of this [impulse forward]. Just as in Beethoven's Fifth Symphony the heart beats in choriambic measures, so here a choriambic leitmotif arises, which becomes a palpable melodic gesture, integrated into various rhythms.' A choriamb is a four-syllable metrical unit in which the first and fourth

---

[30] From the "Translator's Afterward," *Willow Springs,* No. 20, Spring 1987, to my translation of Tsvetaeva's cycle "Mileposts II."

syllables are stressed and the second and third are not. In traditional Russian versification, this sequence occurred on the infrequent occasions of trochaic substitution in iambic lines and vice versa. It never had an independent existence. In *After Russia* . . . ., Tsvetaeva made the choriamb her basic metrical building block, using it either unadulterated or in various logaoedic mixtures with iambic or trochaic patterns . . . . [T]he sheer prevalence of such meters in *After Russia* is what gives the poems of this collection an unprecedented sonority."[31]

And here is how Tsvetaeva's Russian reader Brodsky describes what-remains-missing from these translations:

"Oversaturated with stresses, the harmony of Tsvetaeva's verse line is unpredictable; she leans more toward trochees and dactyls than toward the certitude of the iamb.[32] The beginnings of her lines tend to be trochaic rather than stressed, the endings mournful, dactylic. It's hard to find another poet who has made such skillful and abundant use of caesura and truncated feet. In terms of form, Tsvetaeva is significantly more interesting than any of her contemporaries, including the Futurists, and her rhymes are more inventive than Pasternak's. Most importantly, however, her technical achievements

---

[31] Simon Karlinsky, *Marina Tsvetaeva: The Woman, her World and her Poetry* (Cambridge: Cambridge University Press, 1985), 185-186.

[32] Joseph Brodsky describes Tsvetaeva's use of her "signature" meters in the context of "the glut of iambic trimester and tetrameter common to the works of authors belonging both to the 'Harmonic School' and to the Russian Symbolists." Brodsky, op. cit., 209.

have not been dictated by formal explorations but are by-products — that is, natural effects — of speech, for which the most significant thing is its subject."[33]

Despite what-remains-missing in these translations, I've tried to preserve Tsvetaeva's speech, her voice, and her subjects. And, with the very rarest exceptions, these translations preserve Tsvetaeva's "more eccentric punctuation used to express her poetry's hyperbole, and functioning within her work as an active formal marker to gauge her emotion accurately."[34] As poet Tess Gallagher has observed, "The plenitude of dashes and exclamations are important musical scorings[35]" for Tsvetaeva, ". . . . Tsvetaeva's sign of equality (or inequality) — the dash — separates [words] more than a comma would: . . . "[36]

At times, Tsvetaeva uses considerable enjambment (as did Rilke in German in his early work with which she was thoroughly familiar before 1926) so despite her use of rhyme and meter "the thought tends to muscle past the end-line to complete itself in a restless pause at mid-line, and then plunge onward."[37] As Joseph Brodsky has observed: "We needn't look very far" for "her signature, her fingerprint" of "enjambment

---

[33] Brodsky, op. cit., 201.

[34] Olga Peters Hasky, *Tsvetaeva's Orphic Journeys in the Worlds of the Word* (Evanston: Northwestern University Press, 1996).

[35] "Translating the fine excess of spirit in Marina Tsvetaeva," Naydan, op. cit., 13.

[36] Brodsky, op. cit., 206.

[37] "Looking For Rilke, Introduction by Robert Hass," Stephen Mitchell, *The Selected Poetry of Rainer Maria Rilke* (New York: Vintage International, 1989).

extending through the second, third, and fourth lines of '*Novo-godnee*' ["New Year's"].[38]

"But perhaps, precisely because of the frequency of [her use of enjambment], this device did not satisfy her enough, and she felt the need to 'animate' it with parentheses — that minimalized form of lyrical digressing. (In general, Tsvetaeva, like no one else, indulged in the use of typographic means of expressing subordinate aspects of speech).[39]

Another Tsvetaeva signature of note to Brodsky is "the Russian subordinate clause put at the service of Calvinism . . . . Calvinism in the embrace of this subordinate clause . . . [so] it seems there is no more absorbing, more capacious, and more natural form for self-analysis than the one that is built into the multi-stage syntax of the Russian complex sentence."[40]

In making these translations it was impossible to escape an awareness of Tsvetaeva's frequent use of polysemy: "Her virtuosic manipulation of context and the associative capacity of language enable her to engage a panoply of meanings in her texts in very specific ways.[41]" For one notable example, see Tsvetaeva's masterful use of telegraph wires or "lines," whose sagging from pole to pole are "sighs" along the railway "easements" in her much-admired early-Prague cycle of poems to Pasternak, or her use of "trumpets" and "smokestacks" (one and the same word in Russian) in "About Factories."

And, there is everywhere and always her sheer joy in sound – her particular *melopoeia* – which sometimes flashes through

---

[38] Brodsky, op. cit., 212, 214.

[39] Brodsky, op. cit., 214-215.

[40] Brodsky, op. cit., 232-233.

[41] Hasty, op. cit., 23.

(with luck) as in this little bit of early incantation coaxed out of her comb:

> Run a finger lightly — a clicking glissando
> About me alone, and all about me.[42]

In these translations, like Stephen Mitchell's of Rilke,[43] by working as nearly as possible to maintain the content-integrity of her lines, her enjambments, parentheses, dashes, and being sensitive to her models of polysemy, and sound patterning, I've tried to "render exactly" Tsvetaeva's "own sculptural articulation so that it becomes possible for English readers to sense" her "inner stylistic development" and her ways of using the poetic line and "the infinite subordinate clause".[44] As I worked through the final drafts, this arose as the principal difficulty in wrestling with Tsvetaeva's angel, and steadily resolved, and came to rest producing what are, hopefully, faithfully-structured, consistent translations that in effect, preserve Tsvetaeva's *logopoeia*.

> "What appear on the surface to be contradictions and incongruities drive in fact from her highly controlled use of contrasts, paradoxes, and oppositions. In her essentially Hegelian approach, oppositions are not simply synthesized but are shown instead to be products of a circumscribed perspective, which is escaped when the opposition is pressed far enough to reveal its limitations."[45]

[42] White, op. cit., 65.

[43] Mitchell, op. cit.

[44] Brodsky, op. cit., 213.

[45] Hasty, op. cit., 171.

"The general philosophical notions that inform Tsvetaeva's poetry find precise, concrete expression in the material of her art — from minute detail and textual devices of individual poems to the ordering of entire collections. We must not let her Dionysian surface dazzle us. The emotional intensity Tsvetaeva achieves in her verse is the product of highly consistent translations of large poetic concerns into the technical resources of poetry. To appreciate this consistency in her art is to recognize Tsvetaeva as a serious, intellectually responsible thinker whose avant-garde writings document a systematic and sustained engagement with fundamental questions of poetic discourse."[46]

"The definition of poet and poetry that emerges . . . is applied systematically and with impeccable consistency in an impressive demonstration of the potential afforded by analogical thinking, which in Tsvetaeva's system displaces the logical."[47]

Early on in translating Tsvetaeva, I was fortunate to have the help of Tsvetaeva's devoted variorum edition editor, the late Alexander "Sasha" Sumerkin. In working on these newer translations, Sumerkin's scholarly notes written for each of the these lyrics and *poemas* as included in the Russica edition of Tsvetaeva's collected poetry and prose were helpful aids to me, but not nearly as helpful as Sasha himself when he was alive, on the phone frequently, writing letters and notes of explanation and support in

[46] "Preface," Hasty, op. cit., xiv.

[47] Hasty, op. cit., 2.

advance of our phone appointments, as he and I worked together on "Miles I and II," and on my collection of notes for the eventual later translation of "New Year's" as included here.

For these recent translations from *After Russia*, and the three long *poemas* "Poem of the Hill," "Poem of the End," and "New Year's" I've followed the same preparation procedures as before, with the same aims, as foundational work to reading Tsvetaeva's poems — as one poet reading another. In these later translations, I have felt a bit more secure in adding obvious possessives and pronouns (not always explicitly needed in Russian) to support my reading of any given poem as a whole. So, these translations arise, are thrown off, *as the residue of my reading.* I trust that the residue of my reading — as one poet hoping to read another — is the gift to my readers in English, who might otherwise have no opportunity of coming to hear anything of Tsvetaeva's own (still hidden) Russian voice.

First Small-Notebook

It hardly follows that because a poet is a creator, he must be some sort of liar: lie is a word alien to both reason and conscience, while poetic imagination, viewed thoughtfully, concerns how something *could* and *should* be.

– Trediakovsky

1922

BERLIN

* * *

Time I get the message.
In my deaf stupor — time
For those laws of the sublime
Life does telegraph.

Uncertainly — on my shoulders,
My head crowned and pushed on.
Uncertainly — as a solitary ray,
Unnoticed in daylight.

As if from a slack string —
Dust — shaken from my winding-
Sheet. Tribute to my terror
And to my dust's to-dust.

Ardently arbitrary
Time — of silent requests.
Time of our uprooted brethren.
Time of the world's orphaning.

11 June 1922

* * *

Fierce valley,
Valley of love.
Hands: white with salt.
Mouth: black with blood.

A left-breasted Amazon's
Shaft just missed my temple.
Yes — my head on a stone —
Life, who could love you?

To hell with my plans! To hell with my lies!
Here: as a lark, there: as honeysuckle,
Here: by the handfuls: all pitched-out along
With my savageries — and silences,
With my rainbows glimpsed through tears,
With my pilferings, my prevarications . . .

Life, yes, you are a darling!
And greedy too!
You leave your bite-mark
On my right shoulder.

Chirpings in darkness . . .
With the birds I rouse myself!
To leave my own cheerful mark
On your chronicle.

12 June 1922

* * *

Through all the tedious tasks of the day,
During all your arduous convulsions upon her,
You must let fall a few amiable trochees
Of mine, of me, your manly mistress.

Of my sternness' bitter edge,
Of my slight shyness' latent heat,
And of my telegraphic stroke,
Whose name is still — distance.

Same unearthed junk, except: *give me* and *mine,*
Same jealousies, except these, the mundane,
Same verities, — except that *in extremis*
You are still — a Doubting Thomas.

My dear boy! I swear on the grey hair of your predecessors:
I'm a refugee, no one to take under your own roof!
So, long may the left-breasted Amazon's hammerings
Fall upon your most simplistic ends!

Perhaps, amid her twitters and small exchanges
In the eternal strictures of her femininities —
You will call to mind my hand with no rights
Still in its manly sleeve.

My mouth, which seeks no financial gain,
Nor any claim, that might follow later,
My eyes, that manage without lids, without blinking,
To examine still: the light of this world.

15 June 1922

* * *

Так, в скудном труженичестве дней,
Так, в трудной судорожности к ней,
Забудешь дружественный хорей
Подруги мужественной своей.

Ее суровости горький дар,
И легкой робостью скрытый жар,
И тот беспроволочный удар,
Которому имя — даль.

Все древности, кроме: *дай* и *мой,*
Все ревности, кроме той, земной,
Все верности, — но и в смертный бой
Неверующим Фомой.

Мой неженка! Сединой отцов:
Сей беженки не бери под кров!
Да здравствует левогрудый ков
Немудрствующих концов!

Но может, в щебетах и в счетах
От вечных женственностей устав —
И вспомнишь руку мою без прав
И мужественный рукав.

Уста, не требующие смет,
Права, не следующие вслед,
Глаза, не ведающие век,
Исследующие: свет.

15 июня 1922

* * *

Night's whispers: over silk
Your profligate hand.
Night's whispers: over silk
Your insistent mouth.
                              Settling
All the jealousies of the day —
                              and the flaring up
Of all our ancient history — clenched jaw —
And the stifled
Quarrel —
In this rustling . . .

With a leaf
At the window . . .
With the first bird's warble.
— So fine! — And a sigh.
Not that. — You're gone.
I'm gone.
With a flinch
Of my shoulder.

Nothing.
In vain.
An end.
As if not.

And into the vanity of vanities
This sword: the dawn.

17 June 1922

* * *

В стекло . . . Ночные шепота: шелка
Разбрасывающая рука.
Ночные шепота: шелка
Разглаживающие уста.
                    Счета
Всех ревностей дневных —
                    и вспых
Всех древностей — и стиснув челюсти —
И стих
Спор —
В шелесте . . .
И лист

И первой птицы свист.
— Сколь чист! — И вздох.
Не тот. — Ушло.
Ушла.
И вздрог
Плеча.
Ничто
Тщета.
Конец.
Как нет.

И в эту суету сует
Сей меч: рассвет.

17 июня 1922

* * *

Find yourself more credulous lovers,
Who've never rendered wonder into measures.
I know, Venus — is a form of handiwork,
And I am a craftsman — and I know my craft.

Know my range — from High-Church silences
To the baser tramplings of the soul:
The whole length of the sublime ladder — from:
My breath — to: don't dare breathe!

18 June 1922

* * *

Remember this stricture: Earth is
No place to be possessive!
Because later on —
In the City of Friends:

In an empty,
In a severe
Male paradise
— Unbrokenly golden —

In a world where rivers run back,
On the bank — of a river,
I might take into my imaginary hand
The imagined hand of another . . .

A brief spark might crackle,
Burst — meet with answering burst.
(An Apocrypha of hands might
Be concealed in a handshake!)

O there might be a simultaneous drop
Of our clothing, flat as a sword —
In a paradise of male deities,
In a paradise of male victories!

And so, among the adolescents:
Among our equals,

In the fresh latitudes
Of morning, in the great fires

Of these games — on the dry wind
Long live the impassivity of our souls!
In a paradise of Tarpeian cliffs,
In a paradise of Spartan friendships!

20 June 1922

* * *

Помни закон:
Здесь не владей!
Чтобы потом —
В Граде Друзей:

В этом пустом,
В этом крутом
Небе мужском
— Сплошь золотом —

В мире, где реки вспять,
На берегу — реки,
В мнимую руку взять
Мнимость другой руки . . .

Легонькой искры хруст,
Взрыв — и ответный взрыв.
(Недостоверность рук
Рукопожатьем скрыв!)

О этот дружный всплеск
Плоских как меч одежд —
В небе мужских божеств,
В небе мужских торжеств!

Так, между отрочеств:
Между равенств,

В свежих широтах
Зорь, в загараньях

Игр — на сухом ветру
Здравствуй, бесстрастье душ!
В небе тарпейских круч,
В небе спартанских дружб!

20 июня 1922

* * *

When, if ever, dear God,
Will you let fall upon my life
The serenity of grey hair,
The serenity of your altitudes.

When, at last, in the grand silences
Of *those* first light blues
Will my own high shoulder
Have borne all of life.

You, dear God, alone,
Alone, and none of you, know
How I loosed myself from clumps of white
For a deep and mountainous blue.

How beneath a persistent mouth,
Asleep . . . I listened—to the grasses . . .
(Here, in the land of the arts,
Where I pass for a wordsmith!)

And how weary I am grown
Of lies — and the burden of my quit-rent,
As if the last of my muscles
Had turned into the first quiver of a tree . . .

———————

A tree's — first — quiver,
A dove's — first — coo.

(Isn't that your quivering,
Pride, isn't that your coo,
Fidelity?)
   — Stop,
Clear script of penetrating darts!
Of the disappearing ink of love
The sky — it seems — is blank!

If — not — for morning:
Tinkle, and warble, and leaf,
If not for the vanity
Of vanities — ours would have become

Certain lives . . .
    Not a ray, but a scourge —
To the honeysuckle of tender bodies.
With its headlong bounties
The sky — it seems — has its limits!

Day. The cart-road's
Ruts. — I set out. — I'm gone.
A wild and quiet wince
Of my knowing shoulder.

Our masks . . .
    Poured as if out of a pail —
Morning. Whitewash.
Of any trace of a rib
The sky — it seems — is blank!

22-23 June 1922

* * *

The sunburned one has — his ax and plow.
Enough — tribute to dark dustiness!
My hack-working hands allow
These hard-won early hours are precious.

Morning — out of Old Testament darkness —
Everlasting manly prowess!

Out of moss and honey, a smoking fetus —
Be gone — small creature of the early hours!
In the piled furs of somnolence
Sarah — as promised and Hagar —

Heart — cast aside . . .
                — rejoice alike in the mornings'
Everlasting manly prowess!

24 June 1922

* * *

По загарам — топор и плуг.
Хватит — смуглому праху дань!
Для ремесленнических рук
Дорога трудовая рань.

Здравствуй — в ветхозаветных тьмах —
Вечной мужественности взмах!

Мхом и медом дымящий плод —
Прочь, последнего часа тварь!
В меховых ворохах дремот
Сарру-заповедь и Агарь —

Сердце — бросив . . .
— ликуй в утрах,
Вечной мужественности взмах!

24 июня 1922

* * *

Morning! As neither arrow, nor stone:
I! — Liveliest of women:
Life. With both hands
Move into your waking dream.

Yield! (With your forked tongue:
Take me! — You fork-tongued snake!)
Take all of me in my bareheaded
Joy, attach yourself!

Cling! — To today's day on a schooner,
— Cling! — to a slope on skis! — Cling! — to my flaxen head!
Today I wear my newest skin:
My gold-plated, seventh molt!

— Mine! — and what rewards
Has heaven — when in my hands, my mouth:
Life: with its wide-open joy
Greets you in the morning!

25 June 1922

* * *

For some — there are no laws.
At this hour, when our common dream
Is righteous, nearly sacred,
For some there is no sleep:

Let them look — in the innermost-
reticent petal: you are not to be found!

For some — there are no rules:
At this hour, when every mouth
Is dry with the latest betrayals —
For some there is no water:

They torment themselves — with a clenched-
fist — they pound sand!

For some, an unbending —
Life comes at a price.

25 June 1922

* * *

So you will never find me —
In this life — with a sharp and invisible
Fence, I encircle myself.

With honeysuckle, bind myself,
With hoarfrost, cover myself.

So you will never hear me
At night — with a crone's subtlety:
With reticence — I fortify myself.

With rustlings, bind myself,
With silkiness, cover myself.

So you neither flower nor mold in me
Overmuch — in my undergrowth: in my books
I mislay, I bury you, alive:

With fabrications, bind you,
With any pretense, cover you.

25 June 1922

* * *

Дабы ты меня не видел —
В жизнь — пронзительной, незримой
Изгородью окружусь.

Жимолостью опояшусь,
Изморозью опушусь.

Дабы ты меня не слушал
В ночь — в премудрости старушьей:
Скрытничестве — укреплюсь.

Шорохами опояшусь,
Шелестами опушусь.

Дабы ты во мне не слишком
Цвел — по зарослям: по книжкам
Заживо запропащу:

Вымыслами опояшу,
Мнимостями опушу.

25 июня 1922

A BALCONY

Ah, from my revealing declivity —
Down — into dust and black tar!
Given earthly love's half-measure
How many tears, how long — to pickle it?

Balcony. In my salty down-bursts
Black tar of disastrous kisses.
And inescapable hatred's
Sigh: exhausted in a single line!

Squeezed in my fist to a perfect ball —
What: my heart or my torn
Batiste? For these gully-washers
There's a name: — a river, Jordan.

Exactly, since my battle with love
Is wild and hardhearted.
To climb and launch off any granite
Perch — exhausted into death.

30 June 1922

БАЛКОН

Ах, с откровенного отвеса —
Вниз — чтобы в прах и в смоль!
Земной любови недовесок
Слезой солить — доколь?

Балкон. Сквозь соляные ливни
Смоль поцелуев злых.
И ненависти неизбывной
Вздох: выдышаться в стих!

Стиснутое в руке комочком —
Что: сердце или рвань
Батистовая? Сим примочкам
Есть имя: — Иордань.

Да, ибо этот бой с любовью
Дик и жестокосерд.
Дабы с гранитного надбровья
Взмыв — выдышаться в смерть!

30 июня 1922

* * *

Night visitor wandered from home . . .
Sleep and sleep on forever
In the most-tested of refuges,
This insufferable world.

As if — it meant nothing, to tease
My ear! — as your lover — I
Turn away, as if the night were
Sobbing and a cithara — my breast . . .

Here is my lover in his laurels
Who turned all his horses
Out of the hippodrome. The jealousy
Of a god for his favorite.

2 July 1922

* * *

Given the inimitable lies of any life:
Beyond expectation, beyond rumor . . .
Still in the trembling of every muscle
It's possible for you to know: my life!

Even as you lie in the rye: ringing, blue . . .
(Fine, as you lie within lies!) — heat, shaft . . .
Muttering — in the honeysuckle — of innumerable stings . . .
I rejoice, anyway! — You did call!

But don't cross me, my friend, no,
We may have our entanglements, our bodies,
But our souls — are fallen here: nodding into reverie.
Otherwise — why would you sing?

Into the blank book of your silences,
Into the malleable clay of your "yes" —
I'll let you quietly press the shape of my profile:
Since the palm of your hand — is my life.

8 July 1922

* * *

We thought: there would come easier
Days — an untroubled joining of hands.
— With the slap of a single hand,
Friend, let's put an end to this tenderness.

It's not — late yet!
Through chinks — the dawn
(It's not late!) — yet
For us no birds sang.

Be on — your guard!
Let this be our final stake!
No, it's too late now,
Friend, to think of tomorrow!

Let the earth lie lightly upon you!
Friend, upon your very heart!
At our age we can't
Very well put off death!

The dead — at least — can sleep!
Still in my dreams there is no —
Sleep! With the tamp of our shovels,
Friend — let's put an end to this memory!

9 July 1922

* * *

Думалось: будут легки
Дни — и бестрепетна смежность
Рук. — Взмахом руки,
Друг, остановимте нежность.

Не — поздно еще!*
В рас — светные щели
(Не поздно!) — еще
Нам птицы не пели.

Будь на — стороже!
Последняя ставка!
Нет, поздно уже
Друг, если до завтра!

Земля да легка!
Друг, в самую сердь!
Не в наши лета
Откладывать смерть!

Мертвые — хоть — спят!
Только моим сна нет —
Снам! Взмахом лопат
Друг — остановимте память!

_____

* Ударяется и отрывается первый слог.
  Помечено не везде (примеч. М. Цветаевой).

9 июля 1922

* * *

As my hands — rejoin the round
Of the second-hand and marked-down!
Among the many mouths,
And hands, may I not be lost!

Here among the many
Vanities, among whom there is no rest.
I raise my hands,
Friend, to conjure myself back to mind!

So that in these lines
(This dumping-ground of your Highness'!)
You may never wither,
Never come to shrivel as so many here have done.

So that in my breast
(Deep within my thousand-breasted mass
Grave!) — may the rains
Of a thousand years never wear you away . . .

Body among bodies,
— You were my dying twin-starred Narcissus! . . .
May you never come to putrefy
Under that inscription for the lost masses: The Unknown.

9 July 1922

TO BERLIN

Your rain dulls my pain.
Beneath the collapse of shutters going to ruin
I sleep. Hooves along the trembling
Asphalt — like so much applause.

We were so pleased with ourselves — having met.
With our abandon, our golden-mornings.
With our veritable fairy-tale orphan status;
And you had mercy on us, you, ugly pile of buildings!

10 July 1922

БЕРЛИНУ

Дождь убаюкивает боль.
Под ливни опускающихся ставень
Сплю. Вздрагивающих асфальтов вдоль
Копыта — как рукоплесканья.

Поздравствовалось — и слилось.
В оставленности златозарной
Над сказочнейшим из сиротств
Вы смилостивились, казармы!

10 июля 1922

* * *

You'll see for yourself — in time! —
How, cast out on the straw,
She had no need of fame, nor
Of Solomon's treasure.

No, lacing her hands behind her head,
— From her nightingale's throat! —
The Shulamite sang: not of his treasure —
But of his handful of beautiful red-clay!

12 July 1922

* * *

Удостоверишься — повремени! —
Что, выброшенной на солому,
Не надо было ей ни славы, ни
Сокровищницы Соломона.

Нет, руки за голову заломив,
— Глоткою соловьиной! —
Не о сокровищнице — Суламифь:
Горсточке красной глины!

12 июля 1922

* * *

A light-silvery mold
Over brakes and pools.
The curtain breathes — through its opening
A vacillating and diffuse

Light . . . Like falling water on display,
My veil. (Unless I order you — don't move!)
So at times were Persian demons wont to steal
Their favorites from those who slept.

From those with no command of time
— Sleep! — you, who suffer light-headedness.
You, who discount my incantations,
Sleep, as the weaker one, unequal to myself!

Sleep — I remain a fabrication of your mind
From which I soothe away all disparity.
So at times were the Muses wont to come
And make their favorites of certain mortals.

16 July 1922

* * *

Светло-серебряная цвель
Над зарослями и бассейнами.
И занавес дохнёт — и в щель
Колеблющийся и рассеянный

Свет . . . Падающая вода
Чадры. (Не прикажу — не двинешься!)
Так пэри к спящим иногда
Прокрадываются в любимицы.

Ибо не ведающим лет
— Спи! — головокруженье нравится.
Не вычитав моих примет,
Спи, нежное мое неравенство!

Спи. — Вымыслом останусь, лба
Разглаживающим неровности.
Так Музы к смертным иногда
Напрашиваются в любовницы.

16 июля 1922

* * *

The insinuations of your hair:
Of its satiny smoothness, the luster
Of all its tangled strands —

Deep blue midnight, its raven
Color. — To stroke to my heart's content
Tangled all along — the length of my palm.

Poor man! — You needn't credit me!
This is how I pass over your notion,
Your intention: to part — to separate —

The stairs' last creak . . .
This is how I pass over any thorn
On a rose . . . — You needn't prick your hand!

By my consent, in my life so many
Hands. — It's never been easy to tear
My fixed gaze from any shining yoke:

Along the length of your cowlick
I trace its regimentation: black,
I shift it under pressure.

I envy your un-
Yielding palm: the luster
Of your hair, — here, just at your hair-

Line — your eyes . . . Driven into them
Your obstinate notion: this morning's
Delusion — driven beneath your skull!

17 July 1922

* * *

Вкрадчивостию волос:
В гладь и в лоск
Оторопию продольной —

Синь полунощную, масть
Воронову. — Вгладь и всласть
Оторопи вдоль — ладонью.

Неженка! — Не обманись!
Так заглаживают мысль
Злостную: разрыв — разлуку —

Лестницы последний скрип . . .
Так заглаживают шип
Розовый . . . — Поранишь руку!

Ведомо мне в жизни рук
Многое. — Из светлых дуг
Присталью неотторжимой

Весь противушерстный твой
Строй выслеживаю: смоль,
Стонущую под нажимом.

Жалко мне твоей упор-
ствующей ладони: в лоск
Волосы, — вот-вот уж через

Край — глаза . . . Загнана внутрь
Мысль навязчивая: утр
Наваждение — под череп!

17 июля 1922

* * *

Lethe's blindly running sob.
Your debt remitted you: gone
Into Lethe, — barely, barely living
In the murmur of silvery-running willows.

The willows' silvery-Lethean splash
Lamenting . . . Into the blindly-running crypt
Of memories — where I am weary — yoked
To the willows' silvery-Lethean lament.

On my shoulders — the silvery-grey cape
Of an elder, with silvery-dry ivy
On my shoulders — where I am weary — and fallen
Into the blinding, but scented Lethean darkness

Of poppies . . .
                    — and their red color
Faded with age, and their purple — gone grey
In memory, and having drunk all of it —
I run dry.

Tarnishes: my damaged hair's
Thinness, my young Sibyl's
Blindness, my mental lassitude's
Greyness: all seem plated with lead.

Berlin, 31 July 1922

102

PRAGUE

A SIBYL

1

A sibyl: scorched, a sibyl: a standing snag.
Every bird extinct, but the god is near.

A sibyl: drained, a sibyl: a dry spell.
All my veins run dry: but the man is eager!

A sibyl: gone, a sibyl: a yawning maw
Of what is come and gone! — A tree among virgins.

Like a single, sovereign tree in a bare forest —
Like a tree, the fire begins to stir.

Then, under my eyelids — taking flight, unexpectedly,
Out of those dry rivers, the god rises up.

And abruptly, breaking off his search overhead:
His heart and voice go weak: in me!

A sibyl: who speaks! A sibyl: an arc of sky!
So an Annunciation comes to pass at this

Deathless hour, so in the bleached grasses
A perishable virgin becomes the grotto

For a marvelous voice . . .

                                  — so out into the starry vortex
A sibyl: is gone, no longer among the living.

5 August 1922

2

Grey blocks of stone,
Broken faith with our age.
Your body — a grotto
For your voice.

Depths — of night, into your blind
Eyelids, blind loopholes.
A deaf and dumb fortress
Above the various reapers.

Heavy rains stream down
Your shoulders, fungus molds.
A thousand years lap at
Your foot of stunned blocks.

Mountain of sorrow! Under your heavy
Eyelids, in prophetic swarms —
The clay shards
Of kingdoms and the rising dust

Of battles . . .

6 August 1922

3

A SIBYL — TO HER NEWBORN[48]

Latch on
To my breast, my newborn:
Birth — is a falling into days.

From those cliffs beyond the clouds, from nowhere,
My newborn,
How low you are fallen!
Who were spirit, who are now become dust.

Cry, my little one, for them and for us:
Birth — is a falling into time!

Cry, my little one, in the future, and again:
Birth — is a falling into blood,

And into dust,
And into time . . .

Where does the shining of its miracle lie?
Cry, my little one: born into your weight!

Where do the veins of its treasure lie?
Cry, my little one, born into your numbers,

---

[48] This poem is moved here from the future as it seems to belong here.
An original footnote by Tsvetaeva.

And into blood,
And into sweat . . .

But you will come to rise up! For what all the world calls
Death — is a falling into the firmament.

And you will come to see! That what all the world — sees
As eyelids close — is a birth into light.

From this day —
Into eternity.

Death, my little one, is not to sleep, but to rise up,
Not to sleep, but to return.

Swim, my little one! Already the step you push yourself away from
Is fallen behind you . . .
                                            — Rising into the day.

17 May 1923

СИВИЛЛА

1

Сивилла: выжжена, сивилла: ствол.
Все птицы вымерли, но Бог вошел.

Сивилла: выпита, сивилла: сушь.
Все жилы высохли: ревностен муж!

Сивилла: выбыла, сивилла: зев
Доли и гибели! — Древо меж дев.

Державным деревом в лесу нагом —
Сначала деревом шумел огонь.

Потом, под веками — в разбег, врасплох,
Сухими реками взметнулся Бог.

И вдруг, отчаявшись искать извне:
Сердцем и голосом упав: во мне!

Сивилла: вещая! Сивилла: свод!
Так Благовещенье свершилось в тот

Час не стареющий, так в седость трав
Бренная девственность, пещерой став

Дивному голосу . . .
— так в звездный вихрь
Сивилла: выбывшая из живых.

5 августа 1922

2

Каменной глыбой серой,
С веком порвав родство.
Тело твое — пещера
Голоса твоего.

Недрами — в ночь, сквозь слепость
Век, слепотой бойниц.
Глухонемая крепость
Над пестротою жниц.

Кутают ливни плечи
В плащ, плесневеет гриб.
Тысячелетья плещут
У столбняковых глыб.

Горе горе! Под толщей
Век, в прозорливых тьмах —
Глиняные осколки
Царств и дорожный прах

Битв . . .

6 августа 1922

3

СИВИЛЛА — МЛАДЕНЦУ

К груди моей,
Младенец, льни:
Рождение — паденье в дни.

С заоблачных нигдешних скал,
Младенец мой,
Как низко пал!
Ты духом был, ты прахом стал.

Плачь, маленький, о них и нас:
Рождение — паденье в час!

Плачь, маленький, и впредь, и вновь:
Рождение — паденье в кровь,

И в прах,
И в час . . .

Где зарева его чудес?
Плачь, маленький: рожденье в вес!

Где залежи его щедрот?
Плачь, маленький: рожденье в счет,

И в кровь,
И в пот . . .

Но встанешь! То, что в мире смертью
Названо — паденье в твердь.

Но узришь! То, что в мире — век
Смежение — рожденье в свет.

Из днесь —
В навек.

Смерть, маленький, не спать, а встать.
Не спать, а вспять.

Вплавь, маленький! Уже ступень
Оставлена . . .
               — Восстанье в день.

17 мая 1923

* * *

But it's cramped for two
Even in the joy of morning.
Pushing away with my head
And yielding within,

(For my wanderer — Spirit,
Who walks alone),
Through elemental clay, or
However you stop your ears —

Above their source,
Listen-listen, my Adam,
To what my running river
Currents are — to their banks:

You are both way and station,
Both road and home.
With no lands left for us
To discover together.

To the wider world of many
You are both bridge and surge.
(An autocratic — God
And above all, jealous).

Above their source
Listen-listen, my Adam,

To what my running river
Currents are — to their banks:

Beware of keeping a servant,
So that in your father's house
At the proud hour of his trumpet
You not come before him as a slave.

Beware of keeping a woman,
So that, when you shed your dust,
At the naked hour of his trumpet
You not come before him wearing rings.

Above their source
Listen-listen, my Adam,
To what my running river
Currents are — to their banks:

Beware! Don't found your
Hopes on our relationship.
(For firmer — than any *she*
At our heart — is *this*).

I say, don't flatter yourself
You can own an eagle, — even a king
Laments to this day — one fallen
Into Heaven — remember David!

Above their source
Listen-listen, my Adam,

To what my running river
Currents are — to their banks:

Beware these pitfalls:
More empty than whores!
Whatever died was and is
Decomposed: beware sepulchers!

Yesterday's conjugal rights
In our house—stench and grit.
Let their sweepings
Be gone in the winds!

Above their source
Listen-listen, my Adam,
To what my running river
Currents are—to their banks:

Beware . . .

8 August 1922

* * *

Lethe's underwater light,
My red heart's reef.
The lancet caught, as it
Opened my singing throat:

Neither the cautery of our mouths,
Nor the fever of ill will —
Moves the insoluble pearl, lodged
In the bitter flux of our singing throats.

Mountain of sorrow! We cut facets,
Smelt and fade out — to no good end.
Unable to dissolve
In our voices' focused light

That pearl . . .
                    Like iron in the whine
Of a thousand saws and drills —
An un-extracted nail, caught
In the bitter flux of our singing throats.

11 August 1922

TREES

For my Czech friend,
Anna Antonova Teskova.

1

Having lost faith in mortals,
I want no more of enchantment.
Into the late-season heather,
Into the slip-silver of a dry spell,

— Let my shade's name
Go trumpeted by the trumpeters! —
Into the heather-wastes,
Into the heather-dry streams.

Late-season heather!
Bare stone outcrop!
That assure me
We are the same sort of orphan,

Dropping or stripping away
The last shreds of brocade —
Into the heather-ruins,
Into the heather-dry streams.

Life: the duplicity of its affairs
And the strictures of its ugliness.

By greyness and dryness,
(For now my guide is — rigorous),

Led up, where the rowanberry
Stands finer than King-David!
Into the heather-greys,
Into the heather-dry waves.

5 September 1922

2

When down a string of insults — my incensed
Soul has worked its way,
When seven times over I have renounced
Joining battle with my demons —

It's not to these un-subsiding
Heavy rains of fire into an abyss:
Not to any earthly meanness of time,
Not to human stubbornness —

Trees! I come to you! To escape
The roar of the marketplace!
Your upward soaring is
How my heart exhausts itself!

Oak who resists the gods! With your thrashing
And all your roots walking in state!
My willow-prophets!
My birch-virgins!

Elm — a frenzied Absalom,
In torture, up there, on the rack,
Pine — to my lips, you are a psalm:
Bitterness of rowan berries . . .

To you! Into your lively quicksilver
Of leaves — let them all come down!

For the first time I fling my arms wide!
Pitch out my manuscripts!

Your green reflections in swarms . . .
As if splashing — into my arms . . .
My bare-headed ones,
My shivering ones!

8 September 1922

3

Like bathers, in a loose circle
Churning, like a gathering
Of protecting nymphs — then suddenly,
The tossing tree lines

Like thrown-back heads and hands,
— A scroll unwound! —
In their dance come to a sudden end
Like a wave of defenders —

Like a slender arm to a hip . . .
Like a craning neck . . .
The birches' silver,
The lively brooks!

9 September 1922

4

Friends! My gathered brothers!
You, whose wave has swept away
Every trace of earthly insult.
Forest! — My own Elysium!

From the raucous camp of the over-
Familiar boozy companions of my soul
I will come to my end, choosing sobriety,
A day — in your quietest of fraternities.

O, from the threshing floors
Into the bright sacrificial fires
Of your groves! The great repose
Of your mosses! The shedding of your conifers . . .

The tree's prophetic news!
The forest prophesying: There is
Here, above the criminal rabble —
A perfect life:

Without servitude, or ugliness,
Where things take on their full magnitude,
Where truth is accorded greater stature:
On the far side of our days . . .

17 September 1922

5

Deserters? — Adjuncts?
Sound off, if you're alive!
Monks in your saddles,
Who see God in the thickets?

How many rushing sandals!
How many blazing towers!
How many hounds and deer —
In the boiling over of trees!

Forest! Today you are — a rider!
What people call
A plague: with a final
Convulsion of trees —

Here — in his loose robes
A boy, raised on nectar.
Here — abruptly and from the root
A forest breaks for the sky!

No, what else: not snowflakes —
In a flood of dry leaves!
I see: headlong lances,
I hear: hooves of blood!

And with his open raiments
Flying by — who saw?! —
That's Saul following David:
To his own dark-complected death!

3 October 1922

6

With neither paint, nor brush!
Light — is a kingdom, and it is grey.
These red leaves — a lie:
Here is light, trampling color.

Color, trampled by light.
Light — to color, like a heel to my chest.
Isn't this where, isn't this where
The mystery and force and essence

Of the autumnal forest lies?
Above the quiet backwater of time
As if a curtain were drawn
Aside — and menacingly behind it . . .

Were your son, seen
Through a raiment of estrangements —
The words: Palestine
And Elysium rise up suddenly . . .

Pouring . . . Transparency . . .
Through a trembling of fine ornament —
Light, more blessed than death
And — the connection breaks.

———————

Autumnal greyness.
You, apotheosis of Goethe!
Here many have come to agreement,
And even more — have come undone.

So these grey hairs gleam:
Like the ancient heads of a family —
The last son,
The last of seven —

Passing through the last doorways —
The extended luminescence of my hands . . .
(I don't trust color!
Here comes purple — the last servant!)

. . . Already unlike light:
Like some sort of luminescence gleaming . . .
Isn't this, isn't this
How — the connection breaks.

———

Still the deserts gleam.
And — having said more than I can:
The sands of Palestine,
The cupolas of Elysium . . .

8-9 October 1922

7

She who slept untroubled by visions —
Woke and rose up.
Into the austere measures of a psalm,
Like a gradual, visual scale —

Swarms of waking bodies:
Hands! — Hands! — Hands!
Like a host under a rain of arrows,
Ripe for tribulation.

Scrolls unwinding into garments
Of dust, transparent as nets.
Hands, covering the privates,
(Of virgins!) — and the whips

Of elders, who know no shame . . .
Of adolescents — like birds!
Like a cavalry at judgment's trumpet!
A torso above the waist

Worked free of its shroud —
Ascent of a grey-beard:
I am! — Transmigration! — Legion!
Whole nations

Of emigrants! — Into mercy and wrath!
Be aware! — Awake! — Remember!
. . . Several trees running up
A high hill, of an evening.

12 October 1922

8

Someone rides — to mortal victory.
The trees assume — gestures of tragedy.
A Jew's — dance before sacrifice!
The trees assume — tremblings of mystery.

This is — a conspiracy against the Age:
Against authorities, accounts, time, the fractional.
This is — a rent veil:
The trees assume — gestures of epitaph . . .

Someone rides. Heaven — like an entrance.
The trees assume — gestures of triumph.

7 May 1923

9

What intuitions,
What truths,
Stir you,
Streams of leaves?

What frenzied
Sibyl's mysteries —
Stir you,
Make you delirious?

What in your breath?
Still I know — you treat
The injury of Time —
With the coolness of Eternity.

Still like a young genius
You rise up — to discredit
The lie of any witness
By pointing to absence.

So that again, as before,
Earth — *appears* to us.
So that — *under our eyelids*
Designs come to pass.

So, never boast about this
Currency — of miracles!

So that—*under our eyelids*
Mysteries come to pass!

And away with certainty!
And away with urgency!
Into the current! — Into oracles
Of indirect speech . . .

Are these leaves — like leaves?
This Sibyl — grown hoarse?
. . . Landslides of leaves,
Ruins of leaves . . .

9 May 1923[49]

[49] The two last poems are placed here from the future, as they seem to belong here. *An original footnote by Tsvetaeva.*

ДЕРЕВЬЯ

Моему чешскому другу,
Анне Антоновне Тесковой

1

В смертных изверясь,
Зачароваться не тщусь.
В старческий вереск,
В среброскользящую сушь,

— Пусть моей тени
Славу трубят трубачи! —
В вереск-потери,
В вереск-сухие ручьи.

Старческий вереск!
Голого камня нарост!
Удостоверясь
В тождестве наших сиротств,

Сняв и отринув
Клочья последней парчи —
В вереск-руины,
В вереск-сухие ручьи.

Жизнь: двоедушье
Дружб и удушье уродств.

Седью и сушью,
(Ибо вожатый — суров),

Ввысь, где рябина
Краше Давида-Царя!
В вереск-седины,
В вереск-сухие моря.

5 сентября 1922

2

Когда обидой — опилась
Душа разгневанная,
Когда семижды зареклась
Сражаться с демонами —

Не с теми, ливнями огней
В бездну нисхлестнутыми:
С земными низостями дней.
С людскими косностями —

Деревья! К вам иду! Спастись
От рева рыночного!
Вашими вымахами ввысь
Как сердце выдышано!

Дуб богоборческий! В бои
Всем корнем шествующий!
Ивы-провидицы мои!
Березы-девственницы!

Вяз — яростный Авессалом,
На пытке вздыбленная
Сосна — ты, уст моих псалом:
Горечь рябиновая . . .

К вам! В живоплещущую ртуть
Листвы — пусть рушащейся!

Впервые руки распахнуть!
Забросить рукописи!

Зеленых отсветов рои . . .
Как в руки — плещущие . . .
Простоволосые мои,
Мои трепещущие!

8 сентября 1922

3

Купальщицами, в легкий круг
Сбитыми, стаей
Нимф-охранительниц — и вдруг,
Гривы взметая

В закинутости лбов и рук,
— Свиток развитый! —
В пляске кончающейся вдруг
Взмахом защиты —

Длинную руку на бедро . . .
Вытянув выю . . .
Березовое серебро,
Ручьи живые!

9 сентября 1922

4

Други! Братственный сонм!
Вы, чьим взмахом сметен
След обиды земной.
Лес! — Элизиум мой!

В громком таборе дружб
Собутыльница душ
Кончу, трезвость избрав,
День — в тишайшем из братств.

Ах, с топочущих стогн
В легкий жертвенный огнь
Рощ! В великий покой
Мхов! В струение хвой . . .

Древа вещая весть!
Лес, вещающий: Есть
Здесь, над сбродом кривизн —
Совершенная жизнь:

Где ни рабств, ни уродств,
Там, где всё во весь рост,
Там, где правда видней:
По ту сторону дней . . .

17 сентября 1922

5

Беглецы? — Вестовые?
Отзовись, коль живые!
Чернецы верховые,
В чащах Бога узрев?

Сколько мчащих сандалий!
Сколько пышущих зданий!
Сколько гончих и ланей —
В убеганье дерев!

Лес! Ты нынче — наездник!
То, что люди болезнью
Называют: последней
Судорогою древес —

Это — в платье просторном
Отрок, нектаром вскормлен.
Это — сразу и с корнем
Ввысь сорвавшийся лес!

Нет, иное: не хлопья —
В сухолистом потопе!
Вижу: опрометь копий,
Слышу: рокот кровей!

И в разверстой хламиде
Пролетая — кто видел?! —
То Саул за Давидом:
Смуглой смертью своей!

3 октября 1922

6

Не краской, не кистью!
Свет — царство его, ибо сед.
Ложь — красные листья:
Здесь свет, попирающий цвет.

Цвет, попранный светом.
Свет — цвету пятою на грудь.
Не в этом, не в этом
ли: тайна, и сила и суть

Осеннего леса?
Над тихою заводью дней
Как будто завеса
Рванулась — и грозно за ней . . .

Как будто бы сына
Провидишь сквозь ризу разлук —
Слова: Палестина
Встают, и Элизиум вдруг . . .

Струенье . . . Сквоженье . . .
Сквозь трепетов мелкую вязь —
Свет, смерти блаженнее
И — обрывается связь.

———————

Осенняя седость.
Ты, Гётевский апофеоз!
Здесь многое спелось,
А больше еще — расплелось.

Так светят седины:
Так древние главы семьи —
Последнего сына,
Последнейшего из семи —

В последние двери —
Простертым свечением рук . . .
(Я краске не верю!
Здесь пурпур — последний из слуг!)

. . . Уже и не светом:
Каким-то свеченьем светясь . . .
Не в этом, не в этом
ли — и обрывается связь.

———————

Так светят пустыни.
И — больше сказав, чем могла:
Пески Палестины,
Элизиума купола . . .

8 — 9 октября 1922

7

Та, что без видения спала —
Вздрогнула и встала.
В строгой постепенности псалма,
Зрительною скалой —

Сонмы просыпающихся тел:
Руки! — Руки! — Руки!
Словно воинство под градом стрел,
Спелое для муки.

Свитки рассыпающихся в прах
Риз, сквозных как сети.
Руки, прикрывающие пах,
(Девственниц!) — и плети

Старческих, не знающих стыда . . .
Отроческих — птицы!
Конницею на трубу суда!
Стан по поясницу

Выпростав из гробовых пелен —
Взлет седобородый:
Есмь! — Переселенье! — Легион!
Целые народы

Выходцев! — На милость и на гнев!
Види! — Буди! — Вспомни!
 . . . Несколько взбегающих дерев
Вечером, на всхолмье.

12 октября 1922

8

Кто-то едет — к смертной победе
У деревьев — жесты трагедий.
Иудеи — жертвенный танец!
У деревьев — трепеты таинств.

Это — заговор против века:
Веса, счета, времени, дроби.
Се — разодранная завеса:
У деревьев — жесты надгробий . . .

Кто-то едет. Небо — как въезд.
У деревьев — жесты торжеств.

7 мая 1923

9

Каким наитием,
Какими истинами,
О чем шумите вы,
Разливы лиственные?

Какой неистовой
Сивиллы таинствами —
О чем шумите вы,
О чем беспамятствуете?

Что в вашем веяньи?
Но знаю — лечите
Обиду Времени —
Прохладой Вечности.

Но юным гением
Восстав — порочите
Ложь лицезрения
Перстом заочности.

Чтоб вновь, как некогда,
Земля — казалась нам.
Чтобы под веками
Свершались замыслы.

Чтобы монетами
Чудес — не чваниться!

Чтобы под веками
Свершались таинства!

И прочь от прочности!
И прочь от срочности!
В поток! — В пророчества
Речами косвенными . . .

Листва ли — листьями?
Сивилла ль — выстонала?
. . . Лавины лиственные,
Руины лиственные . . .

9 мая 1923

ABOUT FACTORIES

1

They stand in the laborer's shadow
As smoke-blackened blocks.
The curls of a moving heaven
Toss now above their soot.

Into the lonely vapor of a tea-room
A greasy peaked-cap shuffles.
These outskirts' last smokestack,
A final trumpet, clamors for justice.

Smokestack! Trumpet! From knit brows
A last blast: we are still here!
What death-sentence is this
Last complaint, this final trumpet!

How deeply into your velvet satiety
Their pitiful sounds sink their teeth!
With what buried-aliveness
And dragging-out to slaughter!

And God? — Up to his neck in smoke,
Won't intercede! We wait in vain!
On him — above beds in hospitals
And prisons, he is tacked up.

In mutilation! Of the living flesh!
As it was and as it will be — to
The end.
         — All the singing of the rails,
Where every despair comes to roost:

Factory! Factory! Because it's called
A factory, this black flock lifting.
Get used to the despair of factory
Smokestacks, trumpets — because

The factory calls. And no intercessor
Will come for you then,
When over the last city, the last
Smokestack, a final trumpet, begins to roar.

23 September 1922

2

On human lips the book of eternity
Is not read silently in vain —
At the last, the last of all the common-gates,
Where the grass begins

And truth begins . . . Seated on a stone,
Watching the flocks of birds . . .
The last — the distant — the farthest of all
In the distance — farther away than all . . .

The farthest one . . .
                    Says: I will rise up!
Even though: I am in the grave!
Hard-breathing — judge of our affairs
And slave — to trumpets, to smokestacks.

Who over this city of ordered atrocities,
Of leprous childhoods,
Who into smoky oxides — like an infamous staff
Is risen, like a finger.

The voice of pits and cellars,
— Of heads on weak necks! —
The voice of the orphaned and small,
And of the wicked — affirmed in their wickedness:

All the smoke-cured carcasses, whom
The devil has bought with a bread-crust!

The voice of props and cots,
Of levers and beams.

For whom — there are no left-overs!
Who is himself — a broken shoe!
The voice of all those without voices
Under your lash, — Take that!

The sniggering in your cellars,
Where they root without light.
For whom — there is no refuse:
Who is himself — a tattered rag!

And doesn't dare stir.
Was born — and lies there!
The voice of little seamstresses
In the pouring rains.

The cough in dark laundries,
The itch of lousy jealousy.
The cry, stained with blood:
There, where they love and quarrel . . .

The voice, beating its forehead
Into dust — on Your gentleness,
(Arrogant men without shirts,
Their voice — one I recognize!)

Night after night, an ode
To the splendor of your firmament!

By all — who come by the unlit passage
Into life, and go with a whisper into death . . .

Nearing the last, the last of all the common-gates,
Here, where everyone is justified —
Since none of us have any justice — standing on a stone,
In the lapping of the first grasses . . .

We join the convicts in their howl —
Coming from their hidden tower:
The voice of heaven's truth
Against the truth of earth.

26 September 1922

* * *

These ashes of my treasures:
Of my losses, of my injuries.
These ashes, before which
Granite — falls to dust.

A dove bare and radiant,
Part of no mated pair.
King Solomon's ashes
Over my great vanity.

Sunset-less time's
Terrible whitewash.
Here walks God in my door —
Now the house burnt down!

Still breathing in the rubble,
My ambitions, my mastery,
Like an upright flame
My spirit — rooted in early grey!

Age, it's not that you ever
Betrayed me, behind my back!
This grey — is the triumph
Of my deathless powers.

27 September 1922

* * *

God help us, the smoke!
— Smoke, God, I can live with! But not — damp!
Moving in with the same complaints that
Made others move out of this apartment:

With the same-old lamp, —
Lamp of a beggar, of a student, of a long commute.
If only there were a small tree
For the children! — And what kind of landlord will we have?

Perhaps one who's not too demanding, one
Who takes payment in necklaces, in coins, in dribbles,
Unavoidable as fate
Before turned-out pockets.

And what kind of neighbor will we have?
A bachelor might be nice, well, if he's quiet!
But there's nothing nice
About this, old — warmed by *our* breath

House, saturated throughout!
With *our* mustiness! Like cotton
In my ear — intoning, you will get used to this!
Worn down not by others': but by your own thumb!

If it's old, it's old, if rundown, rundown,
And all of it expensive . . . So consider these: just rooms!
How we come to be born into this world
I'll never know: but *this* is how we die.

30 September 1922

* * *

Спаси Господи, дым!
— Дым-то, Бог с ним! А главное — сырость!
С тем же страхом, с каким
Переезжают с квартиры:

С той же лампою-вплоть, —
Лампой нищенств, студенчеств, окраин.
Хоть бы деревце хоть
Для детей! — И каков-то хозяин?

И не слишком ли строг
Тот, в монистах, в монетах, в туманах,
Непреклонный как рок
Перед судорогою карманов.

И каков-то сосед?
Хорошо б холостой, да потише!
Тоже сладости нет
В том-то в старом — да нами надышан

Дом, пропитан насквозь!
Нашей затхлости запах! Как с ватой
В ухе — спелось, сжилось!
Не чужими: своими захватан!

Стар-то стар, сгнил-то сгнил,
А всё мил . . . А уж тут: номера ведь!
Как рождаются в мир
Я не знаю: но так умирают.

30 сентября 1922

THANK GOD FOR THE RICH

And hereafter, having been warned aforehand,
That between myself and them — lie vast distances!
That I best count myself among the least,
That my place in the world is honorable:

Beneath the wheels of all excess:
At the table of the depraved, of cripples, of hunchbacks . . .
Well, hereafter, from the roof of a bell tower
I declare: I *adore* the rich!

For their root, putrid and loose,
For their weeping-wound from the cradle,
For their perplexing habit of taking
More from my pocket into their pocket.

For the quietest application of their lips,
Never executed without fanfare.
Since they are not permitted to enter paradise,
Since they won't look me in the eye.

For their secrets — delivered solely by courier!
For their billets doux — delivered solely by messenger!
For the nights thrust upon them,
(As they kiss and drink at will and their leisure!)

Since by calculation, or tedium,
By gold-plate, or yawning, or padding,

They can't get to me, the insolent —
I say: I *adore* the rich!

Despite their being clean-shaven,
Satiated, or drunken (I wink — and overspend!)
Because some — seem suddenly — broken,
Because some hangdog look of theirs

Seems doubtful . . .

               — Isn't this the core
Of non-entity? Are their weights not thumbed?
And because among us lower-classes
There's no — bond of abandonment in this world!

Such an ugly fable:
How camels pass through the eye of a needle.
. . . Because they look, stunned to death,
Excusing themselves, pleading illness,

Or protesting even in bankruptcy . . . "I should lend . . . be glad
Of course" . . .

              Because their quiet word, from pressed lips is:
"I counted his carets, counted on him — as a brother" . . .
I swear: I *adore* the rich!

30 September 1922

ХВАЛА БОГАТЫМ

И засим, упредив заране,
Что меж мной и тобою — мили!
Что себя причисляю к рвани,
Что честно мое место в мире:

Под колесами всех излишеств:
Стол уродов, калек, горбатых . . .
И засим, с колокольной крыши
Объявляю: люблю богатых!

За их корень, гнилой и шаткий,
С колыбели растящий рану,
За растерянную повадку
Из кармана и вновь к карману.

За тишайшую просьбу уст их,
Исполняемую как окрик.
И за то, что их в рай не впустят,
И за то, что в глаза не смотрят.

За их тайны — всегда с нарочным!
За их страсти — всегда с рассыльным!
За навязанные им ночи,
(И целуют и пьют насильно!)

И за то, что в учетах, в скуках,
В позолотах, в зевотах, в ватах,

Вот меня, наглеца, не купят —
Подтверждаю: люблю богатых!

А еще, несмотря на бритость,
Сытость, питость (моргну — и трачу!)
За какую-то — вдруг — побитость,
За какой-то их взгляд собачий

Сомневающийся . . .
　　　　　　　　— не стержень
ли к нулям? Не шалят ли гири?
И за то, что меж всех отверженств
Нет — такого сиротства в мире!

Есть такая дурная басня:
Как верблюды в иглу пролезли.
 . . . За их взгляд, изумленный на-смерть,
Извиняющийся в болезни,

Как в банкротстве . . . «Ссудил бы . . . Рад бы —
Да» . . .
　　　　　　　За тихое, с уст зажатых:
«По каратам считал, я — брат был» . . .
Присягаю: люблю богатых!

30 сентября 1922

GOD

1

Face without aspect.
Serenity. — Charm.
All who share flesh
In you are rehearsed.

Like fallen leaves,
Like loose gravel.
All who make outcry
In you are silenced.

Rime grown over rust —
Over blood — over steel.
All who lie facedown
In you are risen.

1 October 1922

2

Beggars' and doves'
Lonely run of scales.
These would be your
Clothes laid out over
A run of trees?

Groves', copses'.
Books and temples
Restored to us — you rise up.
Like a secret escort
Pine forests rush by:

— Hide them! — Don't betray them!

Using a goose foot
He christened the earth to dream.
Even as an aspen
He rushed by — and pardoned her:
Even for having a son!

Beggars sang:
— Dark, O, dark are the forests!
Beggars sang:
— The last cross is cast off!
God is risen from the churches!

4 October 1922

3

O, there's no fastening him
To your symbols and cares!
He slips through the least chink,
Like the sveltest gymnast . . .

By drawbridges and
Migratory flocks,
By telegraph poles
God — escapes us.

O, there's no schooling him
To stay and accept fate!
In the settled muck of feeling
He — is a grey ice floe.

O, there's no catching him!
Set out on a simple saucer,
God — is no tame begonia
Left to bloom at a window!

Under a vaulted roof all
Wait judgment of their maker.
Whether poets or pilots —
All despair.

Since he's one on the run — who moves.
Since the great starry book of
All: from Alpha to Omega —
Is a trace of his cloak, at best!

5 October 1922

БОГ

1

Лицо без обличия.
Строгость. — Прелесть.
Все ризы делившие
В тебе спелись.

Листвою опавшею,
Щебнем рыхлым.
Все криком кричавшие
В тебе стихли.

Победа над ржавчиной —
Кровью — сталью.
Все навзничь лежавшие
В тебе встали.

1 октября 1922

2

Нищих и горлиц
Сирый распев.
То не твои ли
Ризы простерлись
В беге дерев?

Рощ, перелесков.

Книги и храмы
Людям отдав — взвился.
Тайной охраной
Хвойные мчат леса:

— Скроем! — Не выдадим!

Следом гусиным
Землю на сон крестил.
Даже осиной
Мчал — и ее простил:
Даже за сына!

Нищие пели:
— Темен, ох, темен лес!
Нищие пели:
— Сброшен последний крест!
Бог из церквей воскрес!

4 октября 1922

3

О, его не привяжете
К вашим знакам и тяжестям!
Он в малейшую скважинку,
Как стройнейший гимнаст . . .

Разводными мостами и
Перелетными стаями,
Телеграфными сваями
Бог — уходит от нас.

О, его не приучите
К пребыванью и к участи!
В чувств оседлой распутице
Он — седой ледоход.

О, его не догоните!
В домовитом поддоннике
Бог — ручною бегонией
На окне не цветет!

Все под кровлею сводчатой
Ждали зова и зодчего.
И поэты и летчики —
Все отчаивались.

Ибо бег он — и движется.
Ибо звездная книжища
Вся: от Аз и до Ижицы, —
След плаща его лишь!

5 октября 1922

* * *

So, being still alive, having distributed
Equitably, without offence,
Whatever to whomever can make use of it — this being right,

Slowly Semiramis,
Descending into a pond
Down terraces of untrammeled grasses,
Knowing full well there are
Raiments — more beautiful than those cast off

That come after leaving the waters . . .

7 October 1922

DAYBREAK ON THE RAILS

Meanwhile, as day has yet to break
And set its passions, one against the other,
Out of dampness and wooden sleepers
I will reconstruct my Russia.

Out of dampness — and pilings,
Out of dampness — and greyness.
Meanwhile, as day has yet to break
And no switchman has intervened.

Fog still gives no quarter,
Granite wrapped in canvas
Still rests in its cart,
Checkered fields still not visible . . .

Out of dampness — and flocks . . .
Still despite the frenzied news
The raven-black steel lies —
As Moscow does, beyond the sleepers!

As, under my obstinate eye —
This disembodied estate
Lies flooded to Russia's full
Extent — to triple her expanse!

And — I would open her wider!
Running her more invisible rails,

I swear by her dampness, there roll
Boxcars of those burned out of their houses:

Of those who vanished for good
For God and for the people!
(Boxcars stenciled: forty men
And eight horses).

As, standing between the sleepers,
Distance looms like a cross-arm,
Out of dampness and sleepers,
Out of dampness — and loneliness,

Meanwhile, as day has yet to break
And set its passions, one against the other —
Across the entire horizon
I will reconstruct my Russia!

Without depravity, without lies:
Out of the distance — on two, true deep-blue rails . . .
Hey, here she comes! —Hold on!
Down the line, on far down the line . . .

12 October 1922

1923

* * *

No use singing out to her:
Your cry — a reproach. Your advance
And you — a plunge to the hilt.
To the lowest reaches of an organ's

Unsettling attack — the creative terror
Of invasion — watch out, from these heights
— Every fortress lies at a precipice! —
As you please — let it out like an organ.

But will it resolve? Steel and basalt —
A slope, no, a slip-slide into azure
In your seraphic alto
Breaks into song — into a polyphony of storms.

And this will come to pass! — Watch out! — By
The hundreds others have fallen . . . Listen!
Upon the guttural cry of any singer, I
Wreak my vengeance with an organ's storm!

7 February 1923

* * *

No, no disputing what's true.
Among the cathedral Alps
There's conservatory-glass
Struck by a fledgling alto.

Of a girl or boy:
One on the verge.
One in a thousand —
And already breaking.

Choked at its source:
A hundred and one pearls
Dissolving uselessly
In a vocal stream.

Sing, sing — worlds to their knees!
The choir-master: — That voice
Sings over its blood-kin,
Sings over a Muse!

Of boys' voices, I am
A connoisseur . . . — and in dust and blood
A stream of light scatters
Over the winding-sheet.

No, no telling what's false:
It's not the iridescent fragility, —

But Metastasio's cantata
That harrows my heart.

I swear by God's gifts:
By my living soul! —
More precious to me than any high
Note is your voice as it breaks!

8 February 1923

AN EMIGRANT

Here among you: your lodgings, your lucre, your smoke,
Your ladies, your Legislatures,
Having not got used to you, having not been blunted by you
Like a certain —
Schumann scudding along with spring on the sly:
From above! and beyond!
Like a nightingale's suspended tremolo —
A certain one — is chosen.

The most timorous one, and having stretched him on the rack —
You lick his feet!
Having lost his way among your hernias and love-handles
God is left to wander among your lechers.
Superfluous! Extravagant! Walk-out! Upstart! Uppity
And not grown out of it . . . Unwilling to submit
To the gallows . . . Among your riot of currencies and visas
An exile from Vega — from a distant star.

9 February 1923

MY SPIRIT

Higher! Higher! Hard — to catch a flier!
Without the blessing of her willow —
Like her father's Nereid my spirit pa—ddles,
Like a Nereid into a—zure!

Lyre! Lyre! Caspian's — deep-blue!
Blazon of wings — in the small tent!
Over moths — and — curled spines
Blazon of a double-storm!

Muse! Muse! How is it — you dare?
No more than a knotted bridal veil — fluttering!
Or the wind out of Cossack villages — rustling
Over my pages — washed away, foaming . . .

And meanwhile — bills — pile up,
And meanwhile — hearts and lungs — wheeze,
Simmering — at — a boil
As two frothy — but tempered — wings.

So far above your great — game,
(Among its corpses — and — puppets!)
Not to be pawed over, nor purchased,
Blazing and dan—cing —

Six-winged, and wonderfully cor—dial,
Among your pretenders — prostrated! — utterly,
Unstifled by your carcasses
My spirit – breathes!

10 February 1923

SCYTHIANS

1

From earth to the branch — like lynxes!
From earth to the wind — like whistles!

Written with a goose quill?
No, this would be a Scythian arrow!

Cast by the sharp wing of a vulture
This final pitch-darkness — Scythia!

Friend, don't come down off your horse! No need
To dismount, when the miles — still number in the thousands.
Like an exchange of arrows
When some day by and by — we may exchange letters!

Great — and — silent
Between me and you — Scythia . . .

And sleep, my young, my troubled
Syrian, shot with a mortal arrow
With Laylas — and — lutes
To dull your pain . . .
                              Not for mortal ears —

(Heard once a hundred years)
The epic flight — of Scythia!

11 February 1923

2

(A LULLABY)

Over deep-blue over the steppe
From stars of the Great Dipper
To your forehead, but . . .
      — Sleep,
Deep-blue stifled by pillows.

Breathe, in but not out,
Gaze, don't just glance.
Volynia's-one-eyed-moon,
A Caspian-lullaby.

Over flattery over a walking-stick
Like beads of dew that fall
Fingers begin their work . . .
Footsteps — stifled by pillows

Lie down — but don't move,
Tremble — but don't cry out.
Volynia's-tangled-limbs,
Caspian-caught-in-lies.

From the sea from the Casp-
ian's — deep-blue cape,
An arrow whistled, but . . .
      (sleep,
Death stifled by pillows) . . .

Chase — but don't touch,
Sink in — but don't sink under.
Volynia's-tinkling-chime,
A Caspian—kiss.

13 February 1923

3

From arrows and spells,
From nests and holes,
Goddess Ishtar
Guard my tent:

From brothers, sisters.

From my smelting ore,
From my vat of enmity,
Goddess Ishtar
Guard my quiver . . .

(He took me — the Khan did!)

Let them not linger, the old,
Let them not linger, the ill,
Goddess Ishtar
Guard my fire:

(Its sharp flame!)

Let them not linger — the old,
Let them not linger — the evil,
Goddess Ishtar
Guard my cauldron

(Its glow and resin!)

Let them not linger — the old,
Let them *fall easily* to love — the young!
Goddess Ishtar
Drive my flock
Beyond the dark side of many moons!

14 February 1923

СКИФСКИЕ

1

Из недр и на ветвь — рысями!
Из недр и на ветр — свистами!

Гусиным пером писаны?
Да это ж стрела скифская!

Крутого крыла грифова
Последняя зга — Скифия!

Сосед, не спеши! Нечего
Спешить, коли верст — тысячи.
Разменной стрелой встречною
Когда-нибудь там — спишемся!

Великая — и — тихая
Меж мной и тобой — Скифия . . .

И спи, молодой, смутный мой
Сириец, стрелу смертную
Леилами — и — лютнями
Глуша . . .
              Не ушам смертного —

(Единожды в век слышимый)
Эпический бег — Скифии!

11 февраля 1923

2

(КОЛЫБЕЛЬНАЯ)

Как по синей по степи
Да из звездного ковша
Да на лоб тебе да . . .
— Спи,
Синь подушками глуша.

Дыши да не дунь,
Гляди да не глянь.
Волынь-криволунь,
Хвалынь-колывань.

Как по льстивой по трости
Росным бисером плеща
Заработают персты . . .
Шаг — подушками глуша

Лежи — да не двинь,
Дрожи — да не грянь.
Волынь-перелынь,
Хвалынь-завирань.

Как из моря из Каспий-
ского — синего плаща,
Стрела свистнула да . . .
               (- Спи,
Смерть подушками глуша) . . .

Лови — да не тронь,
Тони — да не кань.
Волынь-перезвонь,
Хвалынь-целовань.

13 февраля 1923

3

От стрел и от чар,
От гнезд и от нор,
Богиня Иштар,
Храни мой шатер:

Братьев, сестер.

Руды моей вар,
Вражды моей чан,
Богиня Иштар,
Храни мой колчан . . .

(Взял меня — хан!)

Чтоб не жил, кто стар,
Чтоб не жил, кто хвор,
Богиня Иштар,
Храни мой костер:

(Пламень востер!)

Чтоб не жил — кто стар,
Чтоб не жил — кто зол,
Богиня Иштар,
Храни мой котел

(Зарев и смол!)

Чтоб не жил — кто стар,
Чтоб нежил — кто юн!
Богиня Иштар,
Стреми мой табун
В тридевять лун!

14 февраля 1923

MY LUTE

Lute! My crazy woman! Without fail,
Driving off the king's demon:
"Her strut before King Saul" . . .
(Not one string, but a convulsion!)

Lute! My wayward woman! Without fail,
Emoting a high-strung regard:
"Her strut before King Saul —
With no call to strike up with fallen angels!"

Sorrow! Like some fisherman I stand
Before an empty pearl-oyster.
This is like pouring molten tin in
To drown a nightingale . . . or worse:

This is my immortal soul poured into the groin
Of the first, kind, young man . . .
This is — no worse than spilling it into blood or dust:
This is — to lose one's voice!

And my lute lost hers! — Go, and be well,
Poor David . . . Lesser places await you!
Having strut before King Saul, my lute
Has no call to strike up — with fallen angels!

14 February 1923

ЛЮТНЯ

Лютня! Безумица! Каждый раз,
Царского беса вспугивая:
«Перед Саулом-Царем кичась» . . .
(Да не струна ж, а судорога!)

Лютня! Ослушница! Каждый раз,
Струнную честь затрагивая:
«Перед Саулом-Царем кичась —
Не заиграться б с аггелами!»

Горе! Как рыбарь какой стою
Перед пустой жемчужницею.
Это же оловом соловью
Глотку залить . . . да хуже еще:

Это бессмертную душу в пах
Первому добру молодцу . . .
Это — но хуже, чем в кровь и в прах:
Это — сорваться с голоса!

И сорвалась же! — Иди, будь здрав,
Бедный Давид . . . Есть пригороды!
Перед Саулом-Царем играв,
С аггелами — не игрывала!

14 февраля 1923

* * *

With winters' plumage
Fanning our unsteady gait —
Come Cherubim
Our infant Marys'!

Into his six-fold wings
Dipping our faces, as if into a pool —
Come Gabriel —
Our beardless groom!

And over our trembling muscles,
And over our babbling, guilty lips,
Come Azrael —
Our final lover!

17 February 1923

A GYPSY'S LAMENT FOR COUNT ZUBOV

Let me break — into shards,
Let me boil — into steam,
Into the strumming of guitars
Let my tongue strum!

Into the fray! Into shaking! Into dust — then not into the fray!
A—ah, a string is broken away!

My man — left,
Left — for Service!
Lam—posts!
Gui—tar frets!

For dust!
For shaking!
Was broken!
Was stricken!

Let my Squeeze-box — be Drugged.
Let my Tongue — Strum.

Into the fray! Into the shaking! Into dust — then not into the fray!
A—ah, a hand is broken away!

From the difficult
From the mercurial
From Zubov —
From you, Sir.

At first light — shaking hands
— Count Zubov, Count Zubov! —
Of all — most gallant Sir!
Count Zu—bov!

Into the fray! Into the shaking! Into the dust — then not into the fray!
A—ah, a soul is broken away!

My shock-troops — fallen!
Lam—posts!
My Army — lost!
Gui—tar frets!

With all — the fallen,
(Not snow — rusty black!)
Teeth pressed — into fur,
E—eh, Count Zubov! . . .

And into dust then and on into . . .

19 February 1923

ПЛАЧ ЦЫГАНКИ ПО ГРАФУ ЗУБОВУ

Расколюсь — так в стклянь,
Распалюсь — так в пар.
В рокота гитар
Рокочи, гортань!

В пляс! В тряс! В прах — да не в пляс!
А — ах, струна сорвалась!

У — ехал парный мой,
У — ехал в Армию!
Стол — бы фонарные!
Ла — ды гитарные!

И в прах!
И в тряс!
И грянь!
И вдарь!

Ермань-Дурмань.
Гортань-Гитарь.

В пляс! В тряс! В прах — да не в пляс!
А — ах, рука сорвалась!

Про трудного
Про чудного
Про Зубова —
Про сударя.

Чем свет — ручку жав
— Зубов-граф, Зубов-граф! —
Из всех — сударь-брав!
Зу — бов граф!

В пляс! В тряс! В прах — да не в пляс!
А — ах, душа сорвалась!

У — пал, ударный мой!
Стол — бы фонарные!
Про — пала Армия!
Ла — ды гитарные!

За всех — грудью пав,
(Не снег — уголь ржав!)
Как в мех — зубы вжав,
Э — эх, Зубов-граф!..

И в прах и в . . .

19 февраля 1923

OPHELIA — TO HAMLET

Like Hamlet — so tightly — laced,
With your halo of dissuasion and knowledge,
Pale — to the last atom . . .
(Being edition — one thousand and what?)

Don't trouble me — with your insolence and shallowness!
(Your adolescent's attic layers of stuff!)
Like some ponderous chronicle
You've already come to lie — on my breast!

Virgin! Misogynist! One who prefers
Quarrelsome spirits! . . . Did it never occur to you
Even once, that — whatever might be plucked
From the little flowerbed of madness . . .

Roses? . . . Don't you know this is — sssh! — The future!
If we pluck them — new ones grow! Have they,
Roses, ever once betrayed us? Like lovers —
Roses, have they ever once betrayed us? — Gone?

Perfused (you with your sweet smell!) you will drown . . .
— Nothing happened! — But we surface in memory
At the hour, when in the rivulet's chronicle
Like Hamlet — tightly-laced — you surface . . .

28 February 1923

ОФЕЛИЯ — ГАМЛЕТУ

Гамлетом — перетянутым — натуго,
В нимбе разуверенья и знания,
Бледный — до последнего атома . . .
(Год тысяча который — издания?)

Наглостью и пустотой — не тронете!
(Отроческие чердачные залежи!)
Некоей тяжеловесной хроникой
Вы на этой груди — лежали уже!

Девственник! Женоненавистник! Вздорную
Нежить предпочедший!.. Думали ль
Раз хотя бы о том — что сорвано
В маленьком цветнике безумия . . .

Розы?.. Но ведь это же — тссс! — Будущность!
Рвем — и новые растут! Предали ль
Розы хотя бы раз? Любящих —
Розы хотя бы раз? — Убыли ль?

Выполнив (проблагоухав!) тонете . . .
— Не было! — Но встанем в памяти
В час, когда над ручьевой хроникой
Гамлетом — перетянутым — встанете . . .

28 февраля 1923

OPHELIA — IN DEFENSE OF THE QUEEN

Prince Hamlet! Enough worm-eaten stuff's
Been stirred up . . . Smell the roses!
Look at me, who — for the sake of a single day —
Counts these as my final hours.

Prince Hamlet! Enough of the queen's heart's
Been called into question . . . It's not for a virgin — to judge
Passion. Phaedra — guiltier by far:
Remains celebrated, down to the present day.

And will be! — But You with Your mixture of lime
And decay . . . Speak, spitefully, as you will with the bones,
Prince Hamlet! Your reason has no reason
To pass judgment on burning blood.

Should you . . . Then beware! . . . Up through
The stories — into her bedchamber — to my heart's content!
I will rise in defense of my queen —
I, who am Your own undying passion.

29 February 1923

ОФЕЛИЯ — В ЗАЩИТУ КОРОЛЕВЫ

Принц Гамлет! Довольно червивую залежь
Тревожить . . . На розы взгляни!
Подумай о той, что — единого дня лишь —
Считает последние дни.

Принц Гамлет! Довольно царицыны недра
Порочить . . . Не девственным — суд
Над страстью. Тяжеле виновная — Федра:
О ней и поныне поют.

И будут! — А Вы с Вашей примесью мела
И тлена . . . С костями злословь,
Принц Гамлет! Не Вашего разума дело
Судить воспаленную кровь.

Но если . . . Тогда берегитесь!.. Сквозь плиты —
Ввысь — в опочивальню — и всласть!
Своей Королеве встаю на защиту —
Я, Ваша бессмертная страсть.

28 февраля 1923

PHAEDRA

1

A COMPLAINT

Hippolytus! Hippolytus! That hurts!
Burns . . . My flaming cheeks . . .
What brutal terror lies hidden
In the name Hippolytus!

Like some long-drawn breaking wave
Along the granite coast.
Burned by Hippolytus!
I swear and rave by Hippolytus!

My arms long to plunge into the earth — to my shoulders!
My teeth long to grind gravel — into dust! . . .
I long to weep and lie down together!
To have my ardent mind catch fire . . .

Come as dust — into my nostrils and lips.
Herculean dust . . . So, I sicken . . . Go blind . . .
Hippolytus, this is worse than being sawn!
This is drier than sand and ash!

Like a horsefly in my open weeping
Wound, lapping there . . . An angry horsefly . . .
This — red wound at a gallop is
A mare on fire!

Hippolytus! Hippolytus! Harness me!
Come into my peplos — as into a crypt.
There is an Elysium — for — old nags:
A knacker's yard! — The horsefly bites!

Hippolytus! Hippolytus! Catch me!
This — into my breast, into my burning source,
Is not your soft-petaled — mouth,
Hippolytus — but a Harpy's beak!

Hippolytus! Hippolytus! Let me drink!
Son and stepson? Ac—complice!
This is lava — not stone
Underfoot! — Is Olympus erupting?

Olympians?! With their sleepy gaze!
Celestial beings — we — molded!
Hippolytus! Hippolytus! In your cloak!
Come into my peplos — as into a crypt!

Hippolytus, appease me . . .

7 March 1923

2

AN EPISTLE

To Hippolytus from Mother — Phaedra — Queen — this news.
To my capricious boy, whose beauty melts like wax
From sovereign Phoebus, and from Phaedra runs . . . So,
To Hippolytus from Phaedra: a moan from my tender lips.

Appease my soul! (Impossible to touch lips
And not appease the soul!) Impossible, pressing myself to your lips,
Not to press myself to Psyche, fluttering guest of the lips . . .
Appease my soul: then, appease my lips.

Hippolytus, how tiresome . . . Shame — is for prostitutes, priestesses!
It's not pure shamelessness cries out for you! Only
Speeches and hands are pure . . . Behind the trembling of lips and hands
Lies a great secret, and silence upon it like a finger.

O pardon me, virgin! half-grown! rider! languor-
Hater! — This isn't lust! Not some caprice of my woman's bo—som!
This is — your own seductress! This is Psyche's adulation —
To hang on your very lips to hear your prattle.

— "For shame!" — But, it's too late. Here comes the final plunge!
My horses have bolted! Off a steep cliff — into the dust —
I am a rider *too!* Then, off the height of my breasts,
Of my fatale two hills into the abyss of your chest!

(Not mine?!) — You'll manage this! Bolder! More tender! More than
Some waxen plank — isn't mine a dark-heart's wax?! —
With your immature stylus make your mark . . . O, let
Hippolytus' secret be read by the lips of your

Insatiable Phaedra . . .

11 March 1923

ФЕДРА

1

ЖАЛОБА

Ипполит! Ипполит! Болит!
Опаляет... В жару ланиты...
Что за ужас жестокий скрыт
В этом имени Ипполита!

Точно длительная волна
О гранитное побережье.
Ипполитом опалена!
Ипполитом клянусь и брежу!

Руки в землю хотят — от плеч!
Зубы щебень хотят — в опилки!
Вместе плакать и вместе лечь!
Воспаляется ум мой пылкий...

Точно в ноздри и губы — пыль
Геркуланума... Вяну... Слепну...
Ипполит, это хуже пил!
Это суше песка и пепла!

Это слепень в раскрытый плач
Раны плещущей... Слепень злится...
Это — красною раной вскачь
Запаленная кобылица!

Ипполит! Ипполит! Спрячь!
В этом пеплуме — как в склепе.
Есть Элизиум — для — кляч:
Живодерня! — Палит слепень!

Ипполит! Ипполит! В плен!
Это в перси, в мой ключ жаркий,
Ипполитова вза — мен
Лепесткового — клюв Гарпий!

Ипполит! Ипполит! Пить!
Сын и пасынок? Со — общник!
Это лава — взамен плит
Под ступнею! — Олимп взропщет?

Олимпийцы?! Их взгляд спящ!
Небожителей — мы — лепим!
Ипполит! Ипполит! В плащ!
В этом пеплуме — как в склепе!

Ипполит, утоли . . .

7 марта 1923

2

ПОСЛАНИЕ

Ипполиту от Матери — Федры — Царицы — весть.
Прихотливому мальчику, чья красота как воск
От державного Феба, от Федры бежит . . . Итак,
Ипполиту от Федры: стенание нежных уст.

Утоли мою душу! (Нельзя, не коснувшись уст,
Утолить нашу душу!) Нельзя, припадя к устам,
Не припасть и к Психее, порхающей гостье уст . . .
Утоли мою душу: итак, утоли уста.

Ипполит, я устала . . . Блудницам и жрицам — стыд!
Не простое бесстыдство к тебе вопиет! Просты
Только речи и руки . . . За трепетом уст и рук
Есть великая тайна, молчанье на ней как перст.

О прости меня, девственник! отрок! наездник! нег
Ненавистник! — Не похоть! Не женского лона — блажь!
То она — обольстительница! То Психеи лесть —
Ипполитовы лепеты слушать у самых уст.

— «Устыдись!» — Но ведь поздно!
Ведь это последний всплеск!
Понесли мои кони! С отвесного гребня — в прах —
Я наездница тоже! Итак, с высоты грудей,
С рокового двухолмия в пропасть твоей груди!

(Не своей ли?!) — Сумей же! Смелей же! Нежней же! Чем
В вощаную дощечку — не смуглого ль сердца воск?! —
Ученическим стилосом знаки врезать . . . О пусть
Ипполитову тайну устами прочтет твоя

Ненасытная Федра . . .

11 марта 1923

EURYDICE — TO ORPHEUS:

To those, who married off the last wisps
Of my winding-sheet (no lips, no cheeks! . . .)
O, didn't it seem he exceeded his grasp,
Orpheus, descending into Hades?

To those, who cast off their last connections
To earth . . . On this final bed of beds
Isn't the great lie of our connection seen,
With insight — as having met the knife.

Already congealed — in all the roses of blood
Over the roomy-cut
Of immortality . . .

                Though you loved me
To the very source of Lethe — I need this peace

Of oblivion . . . For in this spectral house
To those — *you* are the specter, really, and I —
The dead, am real . . . And, I'm saying to you:
— "You need to give this up and go!"

You don't stir me! Nor am I trailing after you!
No hands, see! No lips, on which to press
Your lips! — The serpent's bite of immortality
Has put an end to any womanly ardor.

Already congealed — you can recall my voice! —
Over this final expanse.
No need for Orpheus to descend to Eurydice
And no brothers need trouble their sisters.

23 March 1923

ЭВРЕДИКА — ОРФЕЮ

Для тех, отженивших последние клочья
Покрова (ни уст, ни ланит!..)
О, не превышение ли полномочий
Орфей, нисходящий в Аид?

Для тех, отрешивших последние звенья
Земного . . . На ложе из лож
Сложившим великую ложь лицезренья,
Внутрь зрящим — свидание нож.

Уплочено же — всеми розами крови
За этот просторный покрой
Бессмертья . . .
До самых летейских верховий
Любивший — мне нужен покой

Беспамятности . . . Ибо в призрачном доме
Сем — призрак ты, сущий, а явь —
Я, мертвая . . . Что же скажу тебе, кроме:
— «Ты это забудь и оставь!»

Ведь не растревожишь же! Не повлекуся!
Ни рук ведь! Ни уст, чтоб припасть
Устами! — С бессмертья змеиным укусом
Кончается женская страсть.

Уплочено же — вспомяни мои крики! —
За этот последний простор.
Не надо Орфею сходить к Эвридике
И братьям тревожить сестер.

23 марта 1923

LINES

> The heart's wave would not
> froth up so beautifully, and would not
> become spirit, if, fate, that old
> silent rock, did not oppose it.
>
> *Hyperion,* quoted inexactly,
> Johann Christian Hölderlin (1770-1843)

1

Down a line of humming pillars,
Propping up the Empyrean,
I send you my share
Of earthly dust.
                    Down an avenue
Of sighs — by a line on a pole —
My telegraphic: I lo—o—ve . . .

I implore . . . (no printed form
Will hold it! Using this line is easier!)
These — the pillars, upon which Atlas
Lowered the racetrack
Of the Celestials . . .
                    Down these pillars
My telegraphic: go—o—odbye . . .

Hear this? This is the last stop
In my broken throat: forgi—i—ve . . .

This — rigging above the sea of fields,
The quiet Atlantic path:

Up, up — and we are en—tangled
In Ariadne's: we are re—tur—ned,

And mangled! . . . A charity ward's
Dolor: I'll never get out!
These — in a sendoff of steel
Lines — are the voices of Hades

Distancing themselves . . . Distance
Imploring: Take pi—ty . . .

On me! (From the chorus — can
You make this out?) In the dying clamor
Of obstinate passion is —
The small breath of Eurydice:

Down the embankments — and — ditches
Eurydice's: a—a—las,

Don't lea—

17 March 1923

2

I want to say to you . . . well, no, to put into lines
And squeeze into rhyme . . . My heart's — grown larger!
But still's too cramped, I'm afraid, for the sort of trouble
Found in all of Racine and Shakespeare!

"They each wept, and if blood could ache . . .
They each wept, and if there were snakes — in the roses" . . .
There was just one — for Phaedra — Hippolytus!
Ariadne keened — but just over Theseus!

Torn apart! Leaving no shores or landmarks!
Yes, I can say, having lost count,
That in you I lose all those
Who sometime and somewhere were *fabulous*!

What expectations — when the air is full
Of you — when you take up all the air!
When I am like Naxos — to the bone!
When blood runs under my skin — like the Styx!

Vanity! in me! Everywhere! having closed
My eyes: It's fathomless! no daylight! A date
Lies on the calendar . . .

                        Like you — A rift,
I'm no Ariadne and not able . . .

                              — A loss!

O, over what seas and in what cities
Do I look for you? (The invisible — as the blinded!)
I trust my seeing you off to these lines,
And having come up against this telegraph pole . . . I cry.

18 March 1923

3

(Tracks)

All sorted out and all discarded,
(In particular — your message!)
Wildest of dissonances
Of schools, of thaws . . . (a whole choir

Of help!) Sleeves hoisted
Like banners . . .
                        — Shamelessly! —
These lyrical lines hum
With my high desire.

Telegraph pole! Could anything
Be a more ready choice? So long as the sky remains —
An indisputable transmitter of feeling,
The palpable news of lips . . .

Know, so long as there is a vault to heaven,
So long as there are dawns at the border —
So with clarity and in every part everywhere
And lovingly I will bind you.

Across the ill-starred years of this epoch,
Over mock-embankments — from rigging to rigging —
My un-issued sighs,
My tempestuous passion . . .

Beyond my telegrams (those unregistered
And unfailing urgencies!)
Spring-melt rushes down the drainpipes
To flood the line's expanse.

19 March 1923

4

Well-ordered streets!
Telegraph lines!

Bombastic — lustings — of mine,
A cry — from my gut and onto the wind!
This heart of mine, like a spark
Of magnetism — disrupts the meter.

— "Meter and measure?" But a four—th
Dimension takes vengeance! — Rushing
Above the metrical — this mortal
And false witness — of a whistle!

Ssh . . . So what if (after all aren't there
Lines and poles everywhere?) understanding
Were to dawn on you: the difficulties
Of these utterances — are just the howl

Of a nightingale, run off the rails:
— Without you, beloved, the world is empty! —
Fallen, as I am, in lo—ve with the Lyre
Of your arms, and the Layla of your lips!

20 March 1923

5

I'm no reader of the dark arts! On the white book
Of the River Don's vista I train my eye!
Wherever you are not — there I overtake you,
Pass through you — and haul you back.

In my arrogance, as from a tall cedar,
I survey the world: its vessels swim,
Their lights yaw . . . Out of the sea's depths
I wrench you up — from the bottom!

What you go through for me! When I am everywhere:
I, who am dawns and stones, bread and sigh,
I, who am and will be, and who probe
Your lips — as God probes your soul:

Who breathe — into your hour of hoarseness,
Who drag you through the hedgerows
Of an archangel's judgment! — I, with a mouth full of thorns
And bloodied, haul you back from the dead!

Give up! You know this is no fairy-tale!
— Give up! — This arrow describes its compass . . .
— Give up! — Not one has ever escaped
The one who takes you in without arms:

By breathing . . . (Whose bosom rises,
Whose eyelids are blind, around whose mouth mica—dries . . .)
As a woman of some intuition – I have come to mislead you,
Samuel — and am bound to return alone:

Since another woman is with you, and since on Judgment
Day we will cease to contend . . .
                                        I circle and wait.
I who am and will be, I, who probe
Your soul — as I probe your lips, using my own

To lay you to rest . . .

25 March 1923

6

Hour, when the tsars above
And sacraments move, one to another.
(Hour, when I walk downhill):
Hills come to know.

Designs gather in a circle.
Fates converge: I can't give up!
(Hour, when I see no arms)

Souls come to see.

25 March 1923

7

At the hour my dear brother
Passed the last of the elms
(Those waving, formed up in file),
Tears came — greater than my eyes.

At the hour my dear friend
Rounded the last of a headland
(To mental sighs: return!)
Waves came — greater than my arms.

Indeed my arms — followed you — past my shoulders!
Indeed my lips followed too — to entreat!
Little by little my voice lost volume,
Little by little my wrist lost fingers.

At the hour my dear visitor . . .
— Lord, look at us! —
Tears came greater than the eyes
Of humanity, than the stars
Of the Atlantic . . .

25 March 1923

8

Patiently, as one pounds stone,
Patiently, as one waits to die,
Patiently, as one absorbs news,
Patiently, as one nurses revenge —

I wait for you (fingers laced —
As a consort waits on a Sovereign)
Patiently, as one waits on rhyme,
Patiently, as one worries a cuticle.

I wait for you (eyes — downcast,
Teeth in my lips. Stunned. A paving brick).
Patiently, as one holds off coming,
Patiently, as one strings beads.

Creak of a sledge, answering creak
Of a door: roar of the taiga's winds.
The imperial decree is issued:
— Regime change, entry of a new grandee.

Welcome, then:
Unearthly home that it is —
It *is* my own.

27 March 1923

9

Spring brings on sleep. So, let's sleep.
Even apart, it seems we yield: every piece
Of our broken set unites in sleep.
Maybe we see each other in dreams.

The one who sees it all knows whose
Palm — slips into whose, who — is with whom,
To whom I bring my sorrow,
To whom I confide my everlasting

Sorrow (a child, whose father
Goes unnamed and whose end
Comes unexpectedly!) O, sorrow of those
Who cry with no shoulder to cry on!

Crying over what slips from my fingers
As memory, like a pebble off a bridge . . .
Over all the places already taken,
Over all the hearts already engaged

To servitude — with no break — forever.
Bound to live — a lifetime — without joy!
O, buried — barely able to rise! — at dawn!
Consigned to a shelf, that Elysium of the stunted.

Over how you and I are quieter
Than grass, stone, terror, water . . .
Over the seamstress taking up a hem, left to:
Slave — slave — slave —slave.

5 April 1923

10

I may sleep with others — in rosy tangles
Of tangles . . . For problematical fractions
Of weeks . . .
                    But I will be in you
As a treasure-house of similes

At second-hand — in the sands, gleaned
From detritus, — overheard in the winds,
On the tracks . . . Beyond all the hungry
Outposts, where youth wasted itself.

My shawl — remember it? Drawn tight
In the cold, and hotter than hell
Thrown open . . .
                    Know, that a miracle
Of the heart — lies beneath my skirt, a living creature:

Song! With this firstborn, finer
Than all earlier-born and all Rachels . . .
— My truest heart, caught up in thickets
I overpower with these illusions!

11 April 1923

ПРОВОДА

Des Herzens Woge schaumte nicht
so schon empor empor, und wurde Geist,
wenn nicht der alte stumme Fels,
das Schicksal, ihr entgegenstande.*
Фридрих Гёльдерлин

*Сердечная волна не вздымалась бы
столь высоко и не становилась бы Духом,
когда бы на её пути не вставала
старая немая скала — Судьба (нем).

1

Вереницею певчих свай,
Подпирающих Эмпиреи,
Посылаю тебе свой пай
Праха дольнего.
                По аллее
Вздохов — проволокой к столбу —
Телеграфное: лю — ю — блю . . .

Умоляю . . . (печатный бланк
Не вместит! Проводами проще!
Это — сваи, на них Атлант
Опустил скаковую площадь
Небожителей . . .
                Вдоль свай
Телеграфное: про — о — щай . . .

Слышишь? Это последний срыв
Глотки сорванной: про — о — стите . . .
Это — снасти над морем нив,
Атлантический путь тихий:

Выше, выше — и сли — лись
В Ариаднино: ве — ер — нись,

Обернись!.. Даровых больниц
Заунывное: не выйду!
Это — проводами стальных
Проводов — голоса Аида

Удаляющиеся . . . Даль
Заклинающее: жа — аль . . .

Пожалейте! (В сем хоре — сей
Различаешь?) В предсмертном крике
Упирающихся страстей —
Дуновение Эвридики:

Через насыпи — и — рвы
Эвридикино: у — у — вы,

Не у —

17 марта 1923

2

Чтоб высказать тебе . . . да нет, в ряды
И в рифмы сдавленные . . . Сердце — шире!
Боюсь, что мало для такой беды
Всего Расина и всего Шекспира!

«Все плакали, и если кровь болит . . .
Все плакали, и если в розах — змеи» . . .
Но был один — у Федры — Ипполит!
Плач Ариадны — об одном Тезее!

Терзание! Ни берегов, ни вех!
Да, ибо утверждаю, в счете сбившись,
Что я в тебе утрачиваю всех
Когда-либо и где-либо небывших!

Какия чаянья — когда насквозь
Тобой пропитанный — весь воздух свыкся!
Раз Наксосом мне — собственная кость!
Раз собственная кровь под кожей — Стиксом!

Тщета! во мне она! Везде! закрыв
Глаза: без дна она! без дня! И дата
Лжет календарная . . .

                            Как ты — Разрыв,

Не Ариадна я и не . . .

                            — Утрата!

О, по каким морям и городам
Тебя искать? (Незримого — незрячей!)
Я проводы вверяю проводам,
И в телеграфный столб упершись — плачу.

18 марта 1923

3

(ПУТИ)

Все перебрав и все отбросив,
(В особенности — семафор!)
Дичайшей из разноголосиц
Школ, оттепелей . . . (целый хор

На помощь!) Рукава как стяги
Выбрасывая . . .
                    — Без стыда! —
Гудят моей высокой тяги
Лирические провода.

Столб телеграфный! Можно ль кратче
Избрать? Доколе небо есть —
Чувств непреложный передатчик,
Уст осязаемая весть . . .

Знай, что доколе свод небесный,
Доколе зори к рубежу —
Столь явственно и повсеместно
И длительно тебя вяжу.

Чрез лихолетие эпохи,
Лжей насыпи — из снасти в снасть —
Мои неизданные вздохи,
Моя неистовая страсть . . .

Вне телеграмм (простых и срочных
Штампованностей постоянств!)
Весною стоков водосточных
И проволокою пространств.

19 марта 1923

4

Самовластная слобода!
Телеграфные провода!

Вожделений — моих — выспренных,
Крик — из чрева и на ветер!
Это сердце мое, искрою
Магнетической — рвет метр.

— «Метр и меру?» Но чет — вертое
Измерение мстит! — Мчись
Над метрическими — мертвыми —
Лжесвидетельствами — свист!

Тсс . . . А ежели вдруг (всюду же
Провода и столбы?) лоб
Заломивши поймешь: трудные
Словеса сии — лишь вопль

Соловьиный, с пути сбившийся:
— Без любимого мир пуст! —
В Лиру рук твоих влю — бившийся,
И в Леилу твоих уст!

20 марта 1923

5

Не чернокнижница! В белой книге
Далей донских навострила взгляд!
Где бы ты ни был — тебя настигну,
Выстрадаю — и верну назад.

Ибо с гордыни своей, как с кедра,
Мир озираю: плывут суда,
Зарева рыщут . . . Морские недра
Выворочу — и верну со дна!

Перестрадай же меня! Я всюду:
Зори и руды я, хлеб и вздох,
Есмь я и буду я, и добуду
Губы — как душу добудет Бог:

Через дыхание — в час твой хриплый,
Через архангельского суда
Изгороди! — Все уста о шипья
Выкровяню и верну с одра!

Сдайся! Ведь это совсем не сказка!
— Сдайся! — Стрела, описавши круг . . .
— Сдайся! — Еще ни один не спасся
От настигающего без рук:

Через дыхание . . . (Перси взмыли,
Веки не видят, вкруг уст — слюда . . .)

Как прозорливица — Самуила
Выморочу — и вернусь одна:

Ибо другая с тобой, и в судный
День не тягаются . . .
Вьюсь и длюсь.
Есмь я и буду я и добуду
Душу — как губы добудет уст —

Упокоительница . . .

25 марта 1923

6

Час, когда вверху цари
И дары друг к другу едут.
(Час, когда иду с горы):
Горы начинают ведать.

Умыслы сгрудились в круг.
Судьбы сдвинулись: не выдать!
(Час, когда не вижу рук)

Души начинают видеть.

25 марта 1923

7

В час, когда мой милый брат
Миновал последний вяз
(Взмахов, выстроенных в ряд),
Были слезы — больше глаз.

В час, когда мой милый друг
Огибал последний мыс
(Вздохов мысленных: вернись!)
Были взмахи — больше рук.

Точно руки — вслед — от плеч!
Точно губы вслед — заклясть!
Звуки растеряла речь,
Пальцы растеряла пясть.

В час, когда мой милый гость . . .
— Господи, взгляни на нас! —
Были слезы больше глаз
Человеческих и звезд
Атлантических . . .

26 марта 1923

8

Терпеливо, как щебень бьют,
Терпеливо, как смерти ждут,
Терпеливо, как вести зреют,
Терпеливо, как месть лелеют —

Буду ждать тебя (пальцы в жгут —
Так Монархини ждет наложник)
Терпеливо, как рифмы ждут,
Терпеливо, как руки гложут.

Буду ждать тебя (в землю — взгляд,
Зубы в губы. Столбняк. Булыжник).
Терпеливо, как негу длят,
Терпеливо, как бисер нижут.

Скрип полозьев, ответный скрип
Двери: рокот ветров таежных.
Высочайший пришел рескрипт:
— Смена царства и въезд вельможе.

И домой:
В неземной —
Да мой.

27 марта 1923

9

Весна наводит сон. Уснем.
Хоть врозь, а все ж сдается: все
Разрозненности сводит сон.
Авось увидимся во сне.

Всевидящий, он знает, чью
Ладонь — и в чью, кого — и с кем.
Кому печаль мою вручу,
Кому печаль мою повем

Предвечную (дитя, отца
Не знающее и конца
Не чающее!) О, печаль
Плачущих без плеча!

О том, что памятью с перста
Спадет, и камешком с моста . . .
О том, что заняты места,
О том, что наняты сердца

Служить — безвыездно — навек,
И жить — пожизненно — без нег!
О заживо — чуть встав! чем свет! —
В архив, в Элизиум калек.

О том, что тише ты и я
Травы, руды, беды, воды . . .
О том, что выстрочит швея:
Рабы — рабы — рабы — рабы.

5 апреля 1923

10

С другими — в розовые груды
Грудей . . . В гадательные дроби
Недель . . .
        А я тебе пребуду
Сокровищницею подобий

По случаю — в песках, на щебнях
Подобранных, — в ветрах, на шпалах
Подслушанных . . . Вдоль всех бесхлебных
Застав, где молодость шаталась.

Шаль, узнаешь ее? Простудой
Запахнутую, жарче ада
Распахнутую . . .
        Знай, что чудо
Недр — под полой, живое чадо:

Песнь! С этим первенцем, что пуще
Всех первенцев и всех Рахилей . . .
— Недр достовернейшую гущу
Я мнимостями пересилю!

11 апреля 1923

ARIADNE

1

To be abandoned — is to have inveigled
Into my heart — the deep blue tattoo of seafarers!
To be abandoned — is to be given over
To the seven seas . . . And it's the ninth
Wave, isn't it, sweeps one overboard?

To be given up — is to have been bought
Arduously: night after night after night
Deliriously! O, to blow one's own trumpet is —
To be given up! — This was meant to last and be recalled
As the lips and trumpets of prophesies.

14 April 1923

2

— O with all the voices of shells
You sang to her . . .
                        — With every grass-blade.

— She wearied of the caress of Bacchus.
— Thirsted for the poppies of Lethe . . .

— No matter how salt the sea,
You raced on . . .
                        — Walls fell.
— And she tore her curls out in whole
Handfuls . . .
                        — Into the seafoam they fell . . .

21 April 1923

АРИАДНА

1

Оставленной быть — это втравленной быть
В грудь — синяя татуировка матросов!
Оставленной быть — это явленной быть
Семи океанам . . . Не валом ли быть
Девятым, что с палубы сносит?

Уступленной быть — это купленной быть
Задорого: ночи и ночи и ночи
Умоисступленья! О, в трубы трубить —
Уступленной быть! — Это длиться и слыть
Как губы и трубы пророчеств.

14 апреля 1923

2

— О всеми голосами раковин
Ты пел ей . . .
— Травкой каждою.
— Она томилась лаской Вакховой.
— Летейских маков жаждала . . .

— Но как бы те моря ни солоны,
Тот мчался . . .
— Стены падали.
— И кудри вырывала полными
Горстями . . .
— В пену падали . . .

21 апреля 1923

POEM OF THE GATES

And until the desert of renown
Stops my mouth,
I will sing of bridges and gates,
I will sing of the common places.

And until I lie dead in its snare
I will not be caught up — in human fraud,
I will hit — the most difficult note,
I will sing — to the end of life!

Complaint of trumpets.
Eden of kitchen-gardens.
Spade and rake.
Forelock of the young man.

Day without date.
Willow past bloom.
Life laid bare:
Blood plowed under!

Lathered and thickset,
Lathered and lean:
— Get along, to the square?! —
Like a painting —

Like a painting
Except — also as in the odes:

Uproar of the unemployed,
Uproar of young men.

Hell? – True,
But also a garden — for
Women and soldiers,
Old dogs,
Small children.

"Eden — with quarrels?
With no — shells
Of oysters?
No chandelier?
No applique?!"

— They cried in vain:
To each —
His own.

———————

Here passions run thin and rusty:
With dynamite in hand!
Here, often, conflagrations break out:
The gates burn!

Here hatred runs wholesale and en masse:
With reprisals by machine gun!
Here, often, inundations break in:
The gates float!

Here they weep, here they wail and peal
Into dawning silence.
Here young men under escort
Titter: Don't try that with me!

Here they pay! Here by God and the Devil,
With their backs and their pleas!
Here, as if over a corpse, young men
Mourn themselves.

———————

Here mothers roll over, smothering the baby . . .
— Bridges, sands, crosses on gates! —

Here the youngest is pimped to a shopkeeper, money squandered on
drink . . .
By fathers . . .
         — Bushes, crosses of nettles . . .

— Permit me.
— Forgive me.

23 April 1923

POETS

1

The poet — wanders a roundabout way to speech.
The poet — wanders into the distance by speech.

By planets, by constellations, by a roundabout
Parable's beaten paths . . . Between *yes* and *no*
He swings his arm like a pendulum from a bell tower
To indicate a detour . . . Because the orbits of comets —

Are the poet's orbit. Broken links
Of causality — make his connection! Looking up —
You despair! The poet's eclipses
Arrive unpredicted by the calendar.

He is the one who cuts the cards,
Cheats on weights and measures,
He is the one who *asks* in school,
And beats Kant about the head and shoulders,

Who consigned to a stony grave in the Bastille
Seems to be a tree in all its glory.
The one, whose trail — always grew cold,
The train, that everyone
Misses . . .
           — because the orbit of comets

Is the poet's orbit: seeming to burn, without warmth,
To reap, without having planted — an explosion expanding —
Whose path, long-haired and elliptical,
Arrives unpredicted by the calendar!

8 April 1923

2

In this world there are the superfluous, the accessory,
Uninscribed upon any eye.
(Omitted from your canon,
For them, the dump — is where they come to rest).

In this world there are the hollow, the rattled,
The ones who stand mute — the shit,
The nail — that snags your silken hem!
Mud gone squeamish under the wheel!

In this world there are the pretenders, the invisible:
(Marked: with a leper's spots!)
In this world there are Jobs who
Might envy Job perhaps — were we:

Not poets — coupled with pariahs,
Who having taken the field and flooded the banks
Contend now with all the goddesses for the god,
And with all the gods for the virgin!

22 April 1923

3

What should I do, who am blind and a stepchild,
In this world, where each has a father and sees,
Where like anathemas, along the embankments —
Passions run! where a head-cold is
How I excuse — my weeping!

What should I do, who am by rib and by training
A chorister! — like a line! a sunburn! Siberia!
Pursuing delusions of my own — as if crossing a bridge!
With their weightlessness
In this world of weights.

What should I do, who am a singer and firstborn,
In this world, where the darkest goes — grey!
Where inspiration is bottled, in a flask!
With my excess
In this world of measures?!

22 April 1923

ПОЭТЫ

1

Поэт — издалека заводит речь.
Поэта — далеко заводит речь.

Планетами, приметами, окольных
Притч рытвинами . . . Между да и нет
Он даже размахнувшись с колокольни
Крюк выморочит . . . Ибо путь комет —

Поэтов путь. Развеянные звенья
Причинности — вот связь его! Кверх лбом —
Отчаетесь! Поэтовы затменья
Не предуганы календарем.

Он тот, кто смешивает карты,
Обманывает вес и счет,
Он тот, кто спрашивает с парты,
Кто Канта наголову бьет,

Кто в каменном гробу Бастилий
Как дерево в своей красе.
Тот, чьи следы — всегда простыли,
Тот поезд, на который все
Опаздывают . . .
             — ибо путь комет

Поэтов путь: жжя, а не согревая.
Рвя, а не взращивая — взрыв и взлом —
Твоя стезя, гривастая кривая,
Не предугадана календарем!

8 апреля 1923

2

Есть в мире лишние, добавочные,
Не вписанные в окоём.
(Нечислящимся в ваших справочниках,
Им свалочная яма — дом).

Есть в мире полые, затолканные,
Немотствующие — навоз,
Гвоздь — вашему подолу шелковому!
Грязь брезгует из-под колес!

Есть в мире мнимые, невидимые:
(Знак: лепрозариумов крап!)
Есть в мире Иовы, что Иову
Завидовали бы — когда б:

Поэты мы — и в рифму с париями,
Но выступив из берегов,
Мы бога у богинь оспариваем
И девственницу у богов!

22 апреля 1923

3

Что же мне делать, слепцу и пасынку,
В мире, где каждый и отч и зряч,
Где по анафемам, как по насыпям —
Страсти! где насморком
Назван — плач!

Что же мне делать, ребром и промыслом
Певчей! — как провод! загар! Сибирь!
По наважденьям своим — как по мосту!
С их невесомостью
В мире гирь.

Что же мне делать, певцу и первенцу,
В мире, где наичернейший — сер!
Где вдохновенье хранят, как в термосе!
С этой безмерностью
В мире мер?!

22 апреля 1923

WORDS AND MEANINGS

1

Don't you think about me ever!
(A woman — obsessed!)
Think about me a while: in lines:
Let my distance — last.

Don't you complain about me, say I'm pitiful . . .
Sweeter than most, as they say . . .
On that score, kindly apply: the pedal:
Let my pain — last.

2

Pa — lm to palm:
  — Wh—y be born?
  — No — pity: but kindly:
Let both — distance and pain — last.

3

Distance is drawn out in lines . . .
Distance and pain are a single palm
Peeling itself away — until?
Distance and pain are a single ravine.

23 April 1923

СЛОВА И МЫСЛИ

1

Ты обо мне не думай никогда!
(На — вязчива!)
Ты обо мне подумай: провода:
Даль — длящие.

Ты на меня не жалуйся, что жаль . . .
Всех слаще мол . . .
Лишь об одном пожалуйста: педаль:
Боль — длящая.

2

Ла — донь в ладонь:
— За — чем рожден?
— Не — жаль: изволь:
Длить — даль — и боль.

3

Проводами продленная даль . . .
Даль и боль, это та же ладонь
Отрывающаяся — доколь?
Даль и боль, это та же юдоль.

23 апреля 1923

THE PEDALS

Just as strident as
Distance attenuates.
Longer — longer — longer — longer!
That — is the right pedal.

After a life of pleasantries
To die — aware but without regret.
Softer — softer — softer — softer:
That — is the left pedal.

Memory of a vibrant Kitezh —
Is the right! Let the left
Be Lethean waters: the soft pedal
Sings on past the damper.

Of the provincial, of clique-
isness — incessantly (take note!)
Life has no wish to live . . . and often
Death, no wish to die!

Proclaiming! From all the bare-bone
Keys, laid out in file.
(The left pedal suppresses,
The right pedal prolongs . . .)

Rattling! Like a snake over the un-tuned
Keys, laid out in vibration . . .
Longer, longer, longer, longer
The right pedal goes on lying!

24 April 1923

A PALM

Palms! (handbook of
Youths and virgins).
Who kiss the right,
And read the left.

Entering midnight's
Conspiracy — take care:
Who raises the right,
Conceals the left.

A Sibyl — is the left:
Far from glory.
A certain Scaevola
Serves — for the right.

Still despite hatred
At some widening hour
We offer the world
The left — from the heart!

Still consumed by
Righteous wrath, it is
The right we use to slit
The wrist — *of the left*!

27 April 1923

ЛАДОНЬ

Ладони! (Справочник
Юнцам и девам).
Целуют правую,
Читают в левой.

В полночный заговор
Вступивший — ведай:
Являют правою,
Скрывают левой.

Сивилла — левая:
Вдали от славы.
Быть неким Сцеволой
Довольно — правой.

А всё же в ненависти
Час разверстый
Мы миру левую
Даем — от сердца!

А все же, праведным
Объевшись гневом,
Рукою правою
Мы жилы — левой!

27 апреля 1923

* * *

As steep mountains speak,
As bell towers ring out
A valley's space — my cleft,
A valley's space — my palm.

As all travels freely across azure
As bell towers ring out:
A valley's space — my palm,
A valley's space — my love.

29 April 1923

CLOUDS

1

Broken up — as after a battle
The heavens lie loosened.
The heavens — in furrows.
The embattled heavens.

In migration — as if driven
In driven herds.
The herds — of a shining
Widowed moon!

2

Wait! Isn't that Phaedra's cloak
Under the sky? Aren't those Phaedra's
Carried into the marathons
Of these rushing heavens!

Wait! Isn't that Herodias mounting —
A youth . . . Isn't that a tambourine
Carried on the trumpets of Jericho
Into these bursting heavens!

3

No! A standing wave!
Sank — and proved the prophet right!
A di—vided wave:
The whole sea — in two!

Bea—rds and manes
Moving through the Red Sea!
No! — this is — Judith —
With the head of Holofernes!

May 1, 1923

THIS IS HOW TO LISTEN ATTENTIVELY . . .

1

This is how to listen attentively (to the source
As an estuary would — listen).
This is how to put one's nose into a flower:
Deeply — until that sense is dulled!

How in the air, which is deep blue —
There is a thirst, which is bottomless.
How children, through deep blue sheets,
Are able to stare into the past.

How a young man feels his way into his blood —
Who, until now — was no more than a lotus.
. . . How to fall in love with love:
Sink into its deep abyss.

2

Friend! Don't reproach me for my
Mask, all business, and tame.
This is how to swallow one's pride:
Deeply — until that sense is dulled!

How, working it into the fabric, a weaver
Weaves in a last, vanishing thread.
How children, working themselves into a fit,
Come to whisper into a whisper.

This is how to dance . . . (For God
Who is great — for whom you may whirl!)
How children, winding themselves into a tantrum,
Come little by little to quiet themselves.

This is how blood driven by a sting
Complains — without venom!
How one toys with love:
And then passes: into decline.

3 May 1923

ТАК ВСЛУШИВАЮТСЯ . . .

1

Так вслушиваются (в исток
Вслушивается — устье).
Так внюхиваются в цветок:
Вглубь — до потери чувства!

Так в воздухе, который синь —
Жажда, которой дна нет.
Так дети, в синеве простынь,
Всматриваются в память.

Так вчувствовывается в кровь
Отрок — доселе лотос.
. . . Так влюбливаются в любовь:
Впадываются в пропасть.

3 мая 1923

2

Друг! Не кори меня за тот
Взгляд, деловой и тусклый.
Так вглатываются в глоток:
Вглубь — до потери чувства!

Так в ткань врабатываясь, ткач
Ткёт свой последний пропад.
Так дети, вплакиваясь в плач,
Вшёптываются в шёпот.

Так вплясываются . . . (Велик
Бог — посему крутитесь!)
Так дети, вкрикиваясь в крик,
Вмалчиваются в тихость.

Так жалом тронутая кровь
Жалуется — без ядов!
Так вбаливаются в любовь:
Впадываются в: падать.

3 мая 1923

BROOKS

1

Roaring with prophesies,
With the unrepentant violinist's
Pizzicatos . . . Like scattered beads!
With his Paganinian "Nailed it!"
Overturned . . .

               Notes, planets —
In a downpour!

                — Bring it up!!!

                       — The end . . . To naught . . .

With the untold silences
Speaking garrulously of life:
With Stradivariuses in the nights
The high-water brooks.

4 May 1923

2

Like a necklace, broken
Into a thousand pieces of brass —
Like Zingara in her gold
The village in its brooks.

Awash — in its necklaces!
The hill as it slopes
Skimming like a boat
Into the brooks' honeysuckle.

Like necklaced-harnesses . . .
(Of long-strung shadows
Like necklaces! Like harnesses
Of vanishing horses . . .)

Like necklaced-beads . . .
(Of long-strung coins
Like necklaces! Like beads
Of vanishing planets . . .)

Along cliffs, along hollows,
Both over the face, and into the lap —
Like Zingara in her stolen finery —
The village in its brooks.

To be celebrated in song!
Darkly, passionately
Stealing down on every side
The wandering, gypsy brooks.

6 May 1923

РУЧЬИ

1

Прорицаниями рокоча,
Нераскаянного скрипача
Piccicata'ми . . . Разрывом бус!
Паганиниевскими «добьюсь!»
Опрокинутыми . . .

                Нот, планет —

Ливнем!

      — Вывезет!!!

              — Конец . . . На нет . . .

Недосказанностями тишизн
Заговаривающие жизнь:
Страдивариусами в ночи
Проливающиеся ручьи.

4 мая 1923

2

Монистом, расколотым
На тысячу блях —
Как Дзингара в золоте
Деревня в ручьях.

Монистами — вымылась!
Несется как челн
В ручьёвую жимолость
Окунутый холм.

Монистами-сбруями . . .
(Гривастых теней
Монистами! Сбруями
Пропавших коней . . .)

Монистами-бусами . . .
(Гривастых монет
Монистами! Бусами
Пропавших планет . . .)

По кручам, по впадинам,
И в щеку, и в пах —
Как Дзингара в краденом —
Деревня в ручьях.

Споем-ка на радостях!
Черны, горячи
Сторонкою крадучись
Цыганят ручьи.

6 мая 1923

A WINDOW

On a pleasing Atlantic
Breath of spring —
Like a stupendous butterfly
My curtain — and — I

Like a Hindu widow
Enter the gold-lipped crater,
Like a listless Naiad
Enter the sea beyond a window . . .

5 May 1923

TO HONOR TIME

for Vera Arenskaya

On the refugee-road!
It whooped — and bolted
Headlong on its wheels.
Time! I don't have time.

Caught up in chronicles
And kisses . . . like sands
In rustling streams . . .
Time, you let me down!

Of clock-hands and wrinkles'
Furrows — of American
Innovations . . . — Empty jar! —
Time, you give me short measure!

Time, you hand me over!
Like a debauched wife . . . a "new toy"
You drop . . . — "One hour, but it's ours!"

— Your train leaves on a different
Track! . . —

Since I was born *past*
Time! To no purpose and in vain
You resist! Caliph of an hour:
Time! I will pass you by!

10 May 1923

ХВАЛА ВРЕМЕНИ

Вере Аренской

Беженская мостовая!
Гикнуло — и понеслось
Опрометями колес.
Время! Я не поспеваю.

В летописях и в лобзаньях
Пойманное . . . но песка
Струечкою шелестя . . .
Время, ты меня обманешь!

Стрелками часов, морщин
Рытвинами — и Америк
Новшествами . . . — Пуст кувшин! —
Время, ты меня обмеришь!

Время, ты меня предашь!
Блудною женой — обнову
Выронишь . . . — «Хоть час да наш!»

— Поезда с тобой иного
Следования!.. —

Ибо мимо родилась
Времени! Вотще и всуе
Ратуешь! Калиф на час:
Время! Я тебя миную.

10 мая 1923

HIS SISTER

Hell's too small, heaven too small to contain you:
Everyone's already at the point of dying for you.

But to follow your brother, sadly, into the fire —
Really, is that customary? It's not a sister's
Place, to radiate passion!
Really, is it customary to lie in his barrow . . .
With your brother? . .

                      — "He was and is mine! Even if he's rotten!"

— And that's the order of precedence with graves!!!

11 May 1923

СЕСТРА

Мало ада и мало рая:
За тебя уже умирают.

Вслед за братом, увы, в костер —
Разве принято? Не сестер
Это место, а страсти рдяной!
Разве принято под курганом . . .
С братом?..
— «Был мой и есть! Пусть сгнил!»

— Это местничество могил!!!

11 мая 1923

NIGHT

Time the upper reaches are laid bare,
Time you gaze into our souls — as into our eyes.
These — open sluices of blood!
These — open sluices of night!

Our blood surged, like the night
Our blood surged, — like our blood
The night surged! (Upper regions of the ear
Time: a world poured into our ears — as into our eyes!)

The screen of the visible pulled back!
On time's distinct calm!
Time of the ear opening, like an eyelid,
No longer do we have weight, or breathe: we hear.

A world channeled into our endless ear's
Helix: sucking down sounds,
Helix, — our endless soul! . .
(Time, you enter our souls — as you would our arms!)

12 May 1923

TO STEAL . . .

And perhaps, the finest victory
Over time and gravity —
Is to pass, without leaving a trace,
Is to pass, without leaving a shadow

On the walls . . .
                    Finer perhaps — to exact
By refusal? To erase myself from mirrors?
Like: Lermontov moving through the Caucuses
To steal, without disturbing the rock-faces.

And perhaps — the finest amusement
Given the finger of Sebastian Bach
Would be not to trouble the organ's echo?
To collapse, leaving no dust

For the urn . . .
                    Finer perhaps — to exact
By fraud? To write myself out of the latitudes?
Like: Time moving through an ocean
To steal, without disturbing the waters . . .

14 May 1923

ПРОКРАСТЬСЯ

А может, лучшая победа
Над временем и тяготеньем —
Пройти, чтоб не оставить следа,
Пройти, чтоб не оставить тени

На стенах . . .
                    Может быть — отказом
Взять? Вычеркнуться из зеркал?
Так: Лермонтовым по Кавказу
Прокрасться, не встревожив скал.

А может — лучшая потеха
Перстом Себастиана Баха
Органного не тронуть эха?
Распасться, не оставив праха

На урну . . .
                    Может быть — обманом
Взять? Выписаться из широт?
Так: Временем как океаном
Прокрасться, не встревожив вод . . .

14 мая 1923

Second Notebook

Remember the man who, when asked why he took so many pains in an art which could come to the knowledge of so few people, —

"Few are enough for me," he replied. "One is enough for me. None at all is enough for me."

Montaigne

THE DIALOGUE OF HAMLET WITH HIS CONSCIENCE

— She's on the bottom, with the silt
And water-weeds . . . To sleep with them
She left, — but even there, finds no sleep!
— But I loved her
As forty thousand brothers
Could never love her!
                  — Hamlet!

She's on the bottom, with the silt:
Silt! . . And her last adornments are
Caught on the riverbank snags . . .
— But I love her
As forty thousand . . .
                  — Less,
All in all, than a single lover.

She's on the bottom, with the silt.
— But she's who I —
                (*perplexed*)
                        — loved??

5 June 1923

ДИАЛОГ ГАМЛЕТА С СОВЕСТЬЮ

— На дне она, где ил
И водоросли . . . Спать в них
Ушла, — но сна и там нет!
— Но я ее любил,
Как сорок тысяч братьев
Любить не могут!

                — Гамлет!

На дне она, где ил:
Ил!.. И последний венчик
Всплыл на приречных бревнах . . .
— Но я ее любил
Как сорок тысяч . . .

                — Меньше,
Все ж, чем один любовник.

На дне она, где ил.
— Но я ее —

          (*недоуменно*)

                — *любил??*

5 июня 1923,

THE SEAFARER

Rock and rock me, starry boat!
My head is weary of breaking waves!

Too long now I've lost my moorings, —
My head is weary of thinking:

Of hymns — of laurels — of heroes — of hydras, —
My head is weary of pretensions!

Lay me out among grasses and pine-needles, —
My head is weary of wars . . .

12 June 1923

МОРЕПЛАВАТЕЛЬ

Закачай меня, звездный челн!
Голова устала от волн!

Слишком долго причалить тщусь, —
Голова устала от чувств:

Гимнов — лавров — героев — гидр, —
Голова устала от игр!

Положите меж трав и хвой, —
Голова устала от войн . . .

12 июня 1923

THE CREVASSE

How this matter came to an end
Neither love nor friendship can say.
With every passing day you reply less directly,
With every passing day you disappear more deeply.

Until, you're undisturbed by anything now,
— Only the tree riffles its branches —
As if you've fallen into an icy crevasse —
Into my breast, that hurt itself *so* over you!

From the treasure house of images
Here you are — at random — my divination:
As if in a cut-glass coffin, in me, you
Sleep, — in me, as if in some deep wound

You sleep, — the icy aperture is narrow!
The ices, jealous of their corpses:
Ring — armor — seal — and girdle . . .
With no return and no recall.

Widows, why vex Helen with curses!
Isn't Helen's lovely Troy
Burning! To the crevasse's icy, deep
Blue bottom, you sink to your rest . . .

Having been taken in, as Aetna
Took Empedocles . . . Fall asleep, dreamer!
And tell your people, it avails them nothing:
My breast never gives up its dead.

17 June 1923

РАСЩЕЛИНА

Чем окончился этот случай,
Не узнать ни любви, ни дружбе.
С каждым днем отвечаешь глуше,
С каждым днем пропадаешь глубже.

Так, ничем уже не волнуем,
— Только дерево ветви зыблет —
Как в расщелину ледяную —
В грудь, что так о тебя расшиблась!

Из сокровищницы подобий
Вот тебе — наугад — гаданье:
Ты во мне как в хрустальном гробе
Спишь, — во мне как в глубокой ране

Спишь, — тесна ледяная прорезь!
Льды к своим мертвецам ревнивы:
Перстень — панцирь — печать — и пояс . . .
Без возврата и без отзыва.

Зря Елену клянете, вдовы!
Не Елениной красной Трои
Огнь! Расщелины ледниковой
Синь, на дне опочиешь коей . . .

Сочетавшись с тобой, как Этна
С Эмпедоклом . . . Усни, сновидец!
А домашним скажи, что тщетно:
Грудь своих мертвецов не выдаст.

17 июня 1923

* * *

I'll be late to our fixed
Appointment. Having stopped spring
In time, into the bargain — I'll be grey.
You set too much store on this!

I'll walk for years — and never falter
In my Ophelia's taste for bitter rue!
I'll walk through hills — and hayricks,
I'll walk through souls — and arms.

How long we live on this earth! This thicket —
Of blood! and every drop — a backwater
But always at the edge of the brook
The face of Ophelia in its bitter grasses.

She, who hoped to taste passion, only
Swallowed silt! — Lies like a sheaf on the gravel!
I have loved you sublimely:
I have buried myself in the sky!

18 June 1923

* * *

Early yet — to no longer be!
Early yet — to no longer burn!
Tenderness! The brutal lash
Of Underworld encounters.

However deep your inclination —
The sky — is a fathomless vat!
O, for such love it's
Early yet — not to feel wounded!

Life is alive with jealousy!
Blood longs to stream
On the ground. Does a widow
Give up her right — to his sword?

Life is alive with jealousy!
Loss is consecrated
To my heart! Does the grass
Give up its right — to his scythe?

The secret thirst of grasses . . .
Every new shoot says: "crush me" . . .
Having loosened my bindings,
My wounds remain — mine!

And unless You suture us
— I bleed! — unless You pack my wound —
Early yet for the frozen reaches
Of the Underworld!

19 June 1923

* * *

Рано еще — не быть!
Рано еще — не жечь!
Нежность! Жестокий бич
Потусторонних встреч.

Как глубоко ни льни —
Небо — бездонный чан!
О, для такой любви
Рано еще — без ран!

Ревностью жизнь жива!
Кровь вожделеет течь
В землю. Отдаст вдова
Право свое — на меч?

Ревностью жизнь жива!
Благословен ущерб
Сердцу! Отдаст трава
Право свое — на серп?

Тайная жажда трав . . .
Каждый росток: «сломи» . . .
До лоскута раздав,
Раны еще — мои!

И пока общий шов
— Льюсь! — не наложишь Сам —
Рано еще для льдов
Потусторонних стран!

19 июня 1923

LUNA — TO THE LUNATIC

Those entwined — remain so.
Then — the climax.
At the hour of final delirium
Don't come round.

The lunatic and the genius
Have no friends.
At the hour of final insight
Don't look in.

I — am your eyes. An owl-like
Eye from the roof.
When you are called by name —
Pay no heed.

I — am your soul: Urania:
A door — to the gods.
At the hour of final union
Don't hesitate!

20 June 1923

THE CURTAIN

With the falling-water of the curtain, like froth —
Like pine branches — like flame — roaring past.
The curtain holds no mystery from the stage:
(You — are the stage: I — the curtain).

With the slumbering thickets (as in the high
Hall — confusion reigns)
I conceal the hero in his struggle with Fate,
The place of action — and — the hour.

With the falling-water of rainbows, with the avalanche
Of laurels (you put yourself in my hands! you knew!)
I screen you from the hall,
(I enchant — the hall!)

The mystery of the curtain! A slumbering forest
Of sleeping draughts, grasses, kernels . . .
(Behind the already-shuddering scrim
The entrance of tragedy — like — a storm!)

The box seats, in tears! The balcony, in alarm!
The time is come! The hero is coming!
The curtain moves — like — a sail,
The curtain moves — like — a breast.

From the last heart, o my depths,
I shield you. — The outburst!

Over a st—ung — Phaedra
The curtain rose — like — a vulture.

Here! Rend it! Look! Leaking, is it?
Prepare — the vat!
I will give my royal blood to the last drop!
(A spectator goes white, the curtain glows.)

And then, like a compassionate veil
Drawn over a valley, roaring past like a banner.
The curtain holds no mystery — from the hall.
(The hall — is life, I — the curtain).

23 June 1923

* * *

Mother Superior of strings — I'll take this
In hand, as well. Wait a while
Before falling apart! (This June
You cry, you are — rains!)

And if we have thunder — over our roofs,
Rain — in the house, an unending — downpour —
Well, it's you who writes me a letter,
That you won't send.

You with the spatter of brooks' voices
Who furrow my brain, like lines of poetry.
(Your most voluminous letters
Boxes — won't contain them!)

You, your brow surveying the distances,
Come suddenly over the fields — like a flail
Of silver . . . (Can you not stop?
Child! You'll ruin the crop!)

30 June 1923

THE SAHARA

My handsome ones, don't ride off!
Muffled by sands,
Don't go missing in action where
No soul can say.

In my vain reconnaissance,
My handsome ones, I never lie!
The missing one has come to rest
In his secure coffin.

By poetry as if into countries
Of miracles and fire,
By poetry — as if into countries
He rode into me:

Dry, sandy,
Bottomless and boundless.
By poetry — as if into countries
He sank into me.

Listen free of envy
To this tale of two souls.
Into the oases of his eyes —
Came a sandy dryness . . .

His Adam's apple
Shuddered in appeal . . .

I gripped it tightly,
Like passion and like God.

Nameless — he sank!
Never to be found! Taken.
Deserts without memory, —
In which thousands sleep!

Subsided in the boiling up
Of raging waves. —
Covered in sands,
The Sahara is — your tomb.

3 July 1923

САХАРА

Красавцы, не ездите!
Песками глуша,
Пропавшего без вести
Не скажет душа.

Напрасные поиски,
Красавцы, не лгу!
Пропавший покоится
В надежном гробу.

Стихами как странами
Чудес и огня,
Стихами — как странами
Он въехал в меня:

Сухую, песчаную,
Без дна и без дня.
Стихами — как странами
Он канул в меня.

Внимайте без зависти
Сей повести душ.
В глазные оазисы —
Песчаная сушь . . .

Адамова яблока
Взывающий вздрог . . .

Взяла его наглухо,
Как страсть и как Бог.

Без имени — канувший!
Не сыщете! Взят.
Пустыни беспамятны, —
В них тысячи спят!

Стиханье до кипени
Вскипающих волн. —
Песками засыпанный,
Сахара — твой холм.

3 июля 1923

THE RAILS

In a certain ruled notebook
Luxuriating as if upon linen —
These permanent easements lie,
Like rails, as a deep, cutting blue!

Pushkin's demons: how many, and where
Were they driven! (Passed now — without singing!)
They are leaving — deserting,
They grow cold — lose touch.

Or — remain. Pain like
A rising note . . . Rising
Above love . . . Like Lot's wife
Or poles frozen in an embankment . . .

The hour, when as desperately as any
Matchmaker spreading the sheets. — I'm yours! —
And Sappho, having lost her speaking voice,
Cries like a common seamstress.

A cry of submission! The cry of a marsh
Heron, prescient . . . The depth
Of these permanent easements,
Their sharp whistle, like scissors.

Hopeless red spot,
Spread like a hopeless dawn!
. . . Now and then young women
Are tempted by such linen.

10 July 1923

РЕЛЬСЫ

В некой разлинованности нотной
Нежась наподобие простынь —
Железнодорожные полотна,
Рельсовая режущая синь!

Пушкинское: сколько их, куда их
Гонит! (Миновало — не поют!)
Это уезжают-покидают,
Это остывают-отстают.

Это — остаются. Боль как нота
Высящаяся . . . Поверх любви
Высящаяся . . . Женою Лота
Насыпью застывшие столбы . . .

Час, когда отчаяньем как свахой
Простыни разостланы. — Твоя! —
И обезголосившая Сафо
Плачет как последняя швея.

Плач безропотности! Плач болотной
Цапли, знающей уже . . . Глубок
Железнодорожные полотна
Ножницами режущий гудок.

Растекись напрасною зарею
Красное напрасное пятно!
. . . Молодые женщины порою
Льстятся на такое полотно.

10 июля 1923

MY BROTHER

Scorching, as hot tar:
Unendurable a second time!
My brother, with so
Strange an admixture

Of discord . . . (Sound
Of a torn branch comes here?)
My brother, suddenly setting
Like so many suns!

My brother, with no other sisters:
Now entirely my own!
Up to your funeral pyre —
My brother, provided: we go

Together to heaven or to hell!
We come to rest — with a wound
Like a rose! (My brother,
You are the gift of hell!)

My brother! Looking back over the ages:
Nothing was stronger than
Our bond. Running back — a river . . .
May come to whisper again

Somewhere, to the stars and wooden sleepers,
— In the open, to no third party! —
What was whispered those nights
By Cesare — to Lucretia.

13 July 1923

БРАТ

Раскалена, как смоль:
Дважды не вынести!
Брат, но с какой-то столь
Странною примесью

Смуты . . . (Откуда звук
Ветки откромсанной?)
Брат, заходящий вдруг
Столькими солнцами!

Брат без других сестер:
Напрочь присвоенный!
По гробовой костер —
Брат, но с условием:

Вместе и в рай и в ад!
Раной — как розаном
Соупиваться! (Брат,
Адом дарованный!)

Брат! Оглянись в века:
Не было крепче той
Спайки. Назад — река . . .
Снова прошепчется

Где-то, вдоль звезд и шпал,
— Настежь, без третьего! —
Что по ночам шептал
Цезарь — Лукреции.

13 июля 1923

THE HOUR OF THE SOUL

1

In the dark night of the soul,
Un-reckoned by any clock,
I gazed into the eyes of a boy,
Un-reckoned in the nights

Of anyone yet, like two ponds
— Unclouded by memory and brimming! —
In repose . . .
                    At this point
Your life begins.

My greying Roman she-wolf's
Gaze, upon my fosterling sees — Rome!
My dreaming motherhood's
Rock face . . . With no name for my

Misadventure . . . Every pall is
Lifted — growing out of my losses! —
Just as once above a bull-rush
Basket there bent a daughter

Of Egypt . . .

14 July 1923

2

In the dark hour of the soul,
In the dark — of night . . .
(The gigantic footstep of the soul,
Of the soul at night)

At that hour, soul, take control
Of those worlds, where you want
To rule — mansion of the soul,
Soul, of that, take control.

Redden your lips, powder
Your lashes — with snow.
(Atlantean sigh of the soul,
Of the soul — into the night . . .)

At that hour, soul, darken
Your eyes, where like Vega
You will rise . . . and let sour,
Soul, the sweetest fruit.

Sour and darken:
Grow up: take control.

8 August 1923

3

There's an hour of the Soul, like the hour of the Moon,
Of an owl — the hour, of mist — the hour, of darkness —
The hour . . . Hour of the Soul — like the hour of the harp-string
Of David through the dreams

Of Saul . . . At that hour, tremble,
Vanity, wipe off your rouge!
There's an hour of the Soul, like the hour of a storm,
Child, and this hour — is mine.

This hour of the innermost depths
Of my breast. — The breaking of a dam!
Of all things breaking loose from their hinges.
Of secrets — breaking from their lips!

From my eyes — all the veils lift! All tracks —
Lead back! On the ruled staves — not —
A note! Hour of the Soul, like the hour of Troubles,
Child, and this hour — strikes.

As my Trouble! — as you call it.
As when, as if lacerated by
A scalpel, children — reproach
Their mother: "Why do we live?"

And she, with her palm, cools
Their fever: "We need to. — Lie down."
Yes, the hour of the Soul, like the hour of the knife,
Child, and this knife — is a blessing.

14 August 1923

AS FOR YOU, I AM INCLINED

Maternally — in a dream — with my ear.
As for you, I am inclined to rumor,
As is my soul — to your suffering: a fever? yes?
As for you, I am inclined to your face,

Measuring the up—per reaches of your forehead.
As for you, I am inclined to your blood,
To your heart, to the sky, — to islands of languor.
As for you, I am inclined to your rivers,

Your eyelids . . . As unconsciousness is blessedly inclined
To a lute, as a stairway to gardens, as is a willow
Branch to receding fence-posts and lines . . .
As for you, I am inclined to *all*

Your stars as is the earth (the ancestral bending
Of stars to a star!) — drawn to the banner
Of laurels on the graves of all who suf—fered.
As for you, I am inclined to your wings,

Your muscles . . . As an owl is drawn to its hollow,
As the cover of darkness draws me to the head
Of my grave, — years I've wanted to go!
As for you, I am inclined to your mouth

As to a spring . . .

28 July 1923

MY SHELL

Out of the leprosarium of falsity and malice
I have roused you and taken you

Up! Out of the dead sleep of headstones —
Into my hands, here into these palms, both of them,

Shell-like — now grow, be calm:
Grow like a pearl in these palms!

O, neither sheikh nor shah may buy
The private joy and private awe

Of my shell! . . . None of the beauties'
Hauteur may touch your innermost places

None may appropriate you, like this
My shell-like innermost vault

Of my unassailable hands . . . Sleep!
Private joy of my longing,

Sleep! Clouding the oceans and shores
Into my shell I take you, as into a mouth:

Right to left and top to bottom —
My shell's cradling home.

My soul will never give you up to the day!
Your every torment stifled, muffled,

Soothed . . . As by a clean palm
Cooling and caressing your latent thunder,

Cooling and growing . . . O, suppose! O, behold!
Like a pearl you will emerge from this abyss.

— You will emerge! — With the first word: be!
My tortured body will make way

Like a shell. — O, wide open, shutters! —
For a mother each torture in its season,

In fairness . . . Provided you escape captivity,
You may swallow an entire ocean instead!

31 July 1923

BY CORRESPONDENCE

That Castalian current,
Reciprocity, is not blocked!
By correspondence: beyond my eye
Lies, a larger reality.

Beyond calling, beyond seeing
Like a certain long la
Between my mouth and temptation
A mile of distance . . .

Blessed are the longitudes,
The latitudes of oblivions and strata!
Whose expanse moves into you
Like a note, like a moan

Prolonging itself in you,
Like an echo of a granite heart
Beating into you:
Don't look and don't listen and don't be —

Not that I need it in black
And white — in chalk on a board!
Nearly beyond range
Of my soul, beyond range of ennui —

. . . . As a literary conceit
A final card is dealt.
Expanse, expanse
Now you are — a blank wall!

4 August 1923

A LETTER

One doesn't wait for a letter like this,
Like one waits for — the letter.
A soft scrap,
Around it a ribbon
Of glue. Inside — a small word.
And happiness. And that's — all.

One doesn't wait for happiness like this,
Like one waits for — the end:
A soldier's salute
And into his chest — the lead
Of three 44's. Into his eyes, red.
And that's that. And that's — all.

No happiness — I'm too old!
My flower is — wind-blown!
Waiting for the courtyard square
And its black muzzles.

(For the square of a letter:
For its ink and magic!)
For mortal rest
No one is too old!

Nor for the square of a letter.

11 August 1923

ПИСЬМО

Так писем не ждут,
Так ждут — письма.
Тряпичный лоскут,
Вокруг тесьма
Из клея. Внутри — словцо.
И счастье. И это — всё.

Так счастья не ждут,
Так ждут — конца:
Солдатский салют
И в грудь — свинца
Три дольки. В глазах красно.
И только. И это — всё.

Не счастья — стара!
Цвет — ветер сдул!
Квадрата двора
И черных дул.

(Квадрата письма:
Чернил и чар!)
Для смертного сна
Никто не стар!

Квадрата письма.

11 августа 1923

A MINUTE

Minute: passing: you will pass!
As both passion and friends pass!
So, let me discard today what —
Tomorrow may — snatch away!

Minute: light-weight! A bagatelle
Giving but short measure, listen:
What never even began
Is ended. So, go lie to, go flatter

Others, ten times over, reproach
Those still susceptible to this case
Of measles. Who are you to make
Change of the sea? A watershed

Of my living soul? O, low water! O, small change!
The most renowned King of Munificence,
Solomon, had no more renowned possession,
Than this inscription: "This, too, shall pass" —

On his signet-ring . . . In retrospect
Who can't weigh the vanity
Of your Arabic clock-faces
And your swinging pendulums?

Minute: swinging! It seems
At a slow — gallop! Grinding us

To dust, rubbish! *You, too, shall pass:*
Minute: thrown to the dogs!

O, how quickly I long to depart this world,
Where pendulums rend my soul,
Where even my oblivion is ruled
By the passing minutes of a missed meeting.

12 August 1923

A BLADE

Between us — a double-edged blade
Is sworn — and in our thoughts does lie . . .
Because there are — ardent sisters!
Because there is — fraternal ardor!

Because there is such a mixture
Of prairies in the wind, such a multitude of lips
Breathing . . . Sword, preserve us
From our two immortal souls!

Sword, torment us, and, sword, transfix us,
Sword, chastise us, but, sword, know,
That there is this sort of extremity
In truth, a roof with this sort of edge . . .

A double-edged blade — to set us apart?
And unite us as well! Rending the cloak,
And so uniting us, stern guardian,
Wound on wound and gristle on gristle!

(Listen! were a star to fall . . .
A captive boy fall off a boat
Into the sea . . . There are islands,
Islands for any sort of love . . .)

A double-edged blade, blue
Plunging in, begins to redden . . . Double-

Edged sword — we push into ourselves.
It will be — best we lie down!

It will be — a fraternal wound!
Like this, under the stars, and not
Innocent of anything . . . So, we are two
Brothers, welded upon a sword!

18 August 1923

КЛИНОК

Между нами — клинок двуострый
Присягнувши — и в мыслях класть . . .
Но бывают — страстные сестры!
Но бывает — братская страсть!

Но бывает такая примесь
Прерий в ветре и бездны в губ
Дуновении . . . Меч, храни нас
От бессмертных душ наших двух!

Меч, терзай нас и, меч, пронзай нас,
Меч, казни нас, но, меч, знай,
Что бывает такая крайность
Правды, крыши такой край . . .

Двусторонний клинок — рознит?
Он же сводит! Прорвав плащ,
Так своди же нас, страж грозный,
Рана в рану и хрящ в хрящ!

(Слушай! если звезда, срываясь . . .
Не по воле дитя с ладьи
В море падает . . . Острова есть,
Острова для любой любви . . .)

Двусторонний клинок, синим
Ливший, красным пойдет . . . Меч

Двусторонний — в себя вдвинем.
Это будет — лучшее лечь!

Это будет — братская рана!
Так, под звездами, и ни в чем
Неповинные . . . Точно два мы
Брата, спаянные мечом!

18 августа 1923

THE LESSON OF THOMAS

No arms, no embrace!
Be gone, cock-and-bull of the souls'
Bombast!
I can't see — the water's surface,
I can't hear — the garden's empty:
He wasn't there.

Circles on the water,
To my ears and eyes —
A stone.
Not here — then nowhere.
Into space, as into a vat
He sank.

Hold on, hold fast!
With all the strength of your muscles
Enlarge yourself!
What else are dreams and psalms!
For Thomas' sake, God
Came into this

World: steel yourself
In disbelief — like a Negro
In the hold.
All the way into his wound — with your arm!
For the likes of these, God
Died.

24 August 1923

НАУКА ФОМЫ

Без рук не обнять!
Сгинь, выспренных душ
Небыль!
Не вижу — и гладь,
Не слышу — и глушь:
Не был.

Круги на воде.
Ушам и очам —
Камень.
Не здесь — так нигде.
В пространство, как в чан
Канул.

Руками держи!
Всей крепостью мышц
Ширься!
Что сны и псалмы!
Бог ради Фомы
В мир сей

Пришел: укрепись
В неверье — как негр
В трюме.
Всю в рану — по кисть!
Бог ради таких
Умер.

24 августа 1923

MAGDALENE

1

Between us lie — ten commandments:
The heat of ten bonfires.
Blood kin recoils,
To me, you — are foreign blood.

In the time of the Gospels
I would have been one of those . . .
(Foreign blood — the most desired
And most foreign of all!)

With all my afflictions I would
Have been drawn to you, spread my — gleaming
Mane! — all its demonic tangles
Combed out, I would have poured oils

Over your feet, and under your feet,
And openly, onto the sand . . .
Passion for sale in the marketplace,
Unloosed — undone!

With the froth of my mouth, the grit
Of my eyes and the sweat of all
My profusion . . . I would have
Bound your feet in my hair, as in furs.

Would have spread myself like a cloth
Under your feet . . . Neither he (nor she!)
You would have spoken to that creature
With its fiery curls: rise up, my sister!

26 August 1923

2

Oils, purchased at three times
Their value, sweat of passion,
Tears, hair, — an unreserved
Outpouring, but that one

Fastened his blessed eye
On her fine dry clay:
— Magdalene! Magdalene!
No need to offer so much of yourself!

31 August 1923

3

I've no quarrel with what you've done,
Darling! — as it's all come to pass.
I was barefoot, and you gave me shoes
In the down-pourings of your hair —
And — your tears.

I've no question at what price, or how
You purchased these oils.
I was naked, and you enclosed me
In the wave of your body —
Like a wall.

I'll touch your nakedness with fingers
Gentler than waters and humbler than grasses.
I was erect, and you bent me
Pressing yourself tenderly to me.

Make a way for me through your hair,
Swaddle me without linen.
— Chrism-bearer! What need have I of chrism?
You've washed me all over
Like a wave.

31 August 1923

МАГДАЛИНА

1

Меж нами — десять заповедей:
Жар десяти костров.
Родная кровь отшатывает,
Ты мне — чужая кровь.

Во времена евангельские
Была б одной из тех . . .
(Чужая кровь — желаннейшая
И чуждейшая из всех!)

К тебе б со всеми немощами
Влеклась, стлалась — светла
Масть! — очесами демонскими
Таясь, лила б масла

И на ноги бы, и под ноги бы,
И вовсе бы так, в пески . . .
Страсть по купцам распроданная,
Расплеванная — теки!

Пеною уст и накипями
Очес и потом всех
Нег . . . В волоса заматываю
Ноги твои, как в мех.

Некою тканью под ноги
Стелюсь . . . Не тот ли (та!)
Твари с кудрями огненными
Молвивший: встань, сестра!

26 августа 1923

2

Масти, плоченные втрое
Стоимости, страсти пот,
Слезы, волосы, — сплошное
Исструение, а тот

В красную сухую глину
Благостный вперяя зрак:
— Магдалина! Магдалина!
Не издаривайся так!

31 августа 1923

3

О путях твоих пытать не буду,
Милая! — ведь все сбылось.
Я был бос, а ты меня обула
Ливнями волос —
И — слез.

Не спрошу тебя, какой ценою
Эти куплены масла.
Я был наг, а ты меня волною
Тела — как стеною
Обнесла.

Наготу твою перстами трону
Тише вод и ниже трав.
Я был прям, а ты меня наклону
Нежности наставила, припав.

В волосах своих мне яму вырой,
Спеленай меня без льна.
— Мироносица! К чему мне миро?
Ты меня омыла
Как волна.

31 августа 1923

A PASSAGE

. . . With the eyes of the executed,
The eyes of their widows and orphans —
These official fortresses
Of unthinkable houses.

The tight-wire
Of a line, ballooning of a shirt.
And a private shyness:
So, does anyone live . . . here?

28 August 1923

* * *

From the roof of the world
This hill slopes down to the sky.
Friend, I love you beyond
Measure — and sense.

Before onlookers I mask you
In cloud! In corrosive ash.
. . . From this hill, as from Troy's
Beautiful red — walls.

Passions: to praise the dead,
To shame — the living.
So the battle came to be
Viewed by King — Priam.

Founda—tions collapsed.
To a glow? Blood? Nimbus?
So Troy came to be
Viewed by all O—lympus.

Still, from her cool recess
A Virgin, lifting her palm . . .
Friend, I love you from on high.
Take notice — and — come up.

30 August 1923

A RAVINE

1

Bottom of — a ravine.
Night — snagged
Fumbling. Shaking pine-needles.

Vows — no need.
Lie down — and I will lie down.
You become vagrant with me.

From our rank bed
To drink — the night, drop by
Thawing drop — to your coughing fit. To your heart's content.

Drink! Spotless —
Darkness! Compliments of —
God: as if you were to prostrate yourself to an abyss.

(The time — what is it?)
Night — through these blinds
To know — know a little. To come to know

The night — as thieves,
The night — as hills.
(Each of us — a Sinai

At night . . .)

10 September 1923

2

You'll never know, what I burn, what I waste
— Our hearts missing a beat —
On your tender, empty, ardent breast,
Dear, proud man.

You'll never know, what nothing-to-do-with-us
Storms' — damage you've kissed away!
No hill, no ravine, no wall, no embankment:
This passage of my soul.

O, don't listen too closely! To my anguished gibberish's
Quicksilver . . . Voice of a brook . . .
You're right to take me blindly. In this victory
Your arms take what they will — to your shoulders!

O, don't look too closely! Under the falling leaves
We ourselves — like them, rush headlong!
You're right to take me blindly. Those are just clouds
Trailing their sidelong downpour!

Lie down — and I will lie down. For good. O, forever, and for good!
Like bodies at war —
Like ranks in file. (As they say, at the bottom of a ravine,
If not — at the bottom of heaven!)

In this mad race of sleepless trees
Someone is bound to be trampled to death.
Your victory — is the rout of a *horde*,
Don't you know, my young David?

11 September 1923

ОВРАГ

1

Дно — оврага.
Ночь — корягой
Шарящая. Встряски хвой.

Клятв — не надо.
Ляг — и лягу.
Ты бродягой стал со мной.

С койки затхлой
Ночь по каплям
Пить — закашляешься. Всласть

Пей! Без пятен —
Мрак! Бесплатен —
Бог: как к пропасти припасть.

(Час — который?)
Ночь — сквозь штору
Знать — немного знать. Узнай

Ночь — как воры,
Ночь — как горы.
(Каждая из нас — Синай

Ночью . . .)

10 сентября 1923

2

Никогда не узнаешь, что жгу, что трачу
— Сердец перебой —
На груди твоей нежной, пустой, горячей,
Гордец дорогой.

Никогда не узнаешь, каких не-наших
Бурь — следы сцеловал!
Не гора, не овраг, не стена, не насыпь:
Души перевал.

О, не вслушивайся! Болевого бреда
Ртуть . . . Ручьёвая речь . . .
Прав, что слепо берешь. От такой победы
Руки могут — от плеч!

О, не вглядывайся! Под листвой падучей
Сами — листьями мчим!
Прав, что слепо берешь. Это только тучи
Мчат за ливнем косым.

Ляг — и лягу. И благо. О, всё на благо!
Как тела на войне —
В лад и в ряд. (Говорят, что на дне оврага,
Может — неба на дне!)

В этом бешеном беге дерев бессонных
Кто-то на смерть разбит.
Что победа твоя — пораженье сонмов,
Знаешь, юный Давид?

11 сентября 1923

ACHILLES ON THE WALL

Drained — taken — overcome —
— Flat on my back! — I will die.
Like Polyxena, who beheld Achilles
There, on the wall —

In red — a bloody tower on the horizon
Of bodies he had laid low.
Like Polyxena praying: "Who is this?"
(And knew — the pyre!)

The united sorcery
Of awe, of love.
Like Polyxena, who beheld the Achaean
And whispered — and —

Do you know that ebb of Atlantean
Blood down my cheeks?
Over an invincible — expanse of no-man's land —
The quaking of our blood.

13 September 1923

АХИЛЛ НА ВАЛУ

Отлило — обдало — накатило —
— Навзничь! — Умру.
Так Поликсена, узрев Ахилла
Там, на валу —

В красном — кровавая башня в плёсе
Тел, что простер.
Так Поликсена, всплеснувши: «Кто сей?»
(Знала — костер!)

Соединенное чародейство
Страха, любви.
Так Поликсена, узрев ахейца
Ахнула — и —

Знаете этот отлив атлантский
Крови от щек?
Неодолимый — прострись, пространство! —
Крови толчок.

13 сентября 1923

THE LAST SAILOR

O you — of all below-line notes
The lowest! — Let's put an end to our quarrel!
Like that consumptive woman, who moaned
All night: ravish me again!

Who wrung her hands, as fights
And close blows and ropes of oaths intruded.
(Her sailor — no longer handsome — slept
As blood dropped on his rum-
   pled pillowcase . . .)
                              And then, bottoms up
With the glass, of crystal and blood
Laughing . . . — and she mistook blood for wine,
And she mistook death for love.

"You sleep. I'm — need to go! No preliminaries, no rehearsals —
Just the curtain! Tomorrow, flat on my back!"
Like that consumptive woman, who begged
Everyone: ravish me

A bit more! . . . (My hands are clean now,
My gaze troubled, fingers stiff . . .)
Like that woman with her sailor — with you, o life,
I haggle: for another minute

Ravish me! . . .

15 September 1923

ПОСЛЕДНИЙ МОРЯК

О, ты — из всех залинейных нот
Нижайшая! — Кончим распрю!
Как та чахоточная, что в ночь
Стонала: еще понравься!

Ломала руки, а рядом драк
Удары и клятв канаты.
(Спал разонравившийся моряк
И капала кровь на мя-
тую наволоку . . .)

А потом, вверх дном
Стакан, хрусталем и кровью
Смеясь . . . — и путала кровь с вином,
И путала смерть с любовью.

«Вам сон, мне — спех! Не присев, не спев —
И занавес! Завтра в лёжку!»
Как та чахоточная, что всех
Просила: еще немножко

Понравься! . . . (Руки уже свежи,
Взор смутен, персты не гнутся . . .)
Как та с матросом — с тобой, о жизнь,
Торгуюсь: еще минутку

Понравься!..

15 сентября 1923

THE CRY OF STATIONS

The cry of stations: don't go!
Of terminals: take pity!
And that of the brief stops:
Not exactly Dante's
Benediction:
"Abandon hope!"
And that of the engines.

Whose iron shuddered
Like the thunder of an ocean wave.
At the tiny ticket-window,
It crossed my mind — they traffic in space?
In seas and dry land?
In perishable meat:
We are meat — not souls!
We are mouths — not roses!
From us? No — *over* us
The wheels carry off our loved ones!

At such and such miles per hour.

Tiny ticket-windows.
Little dice of passionate chance.
One of us was right,
Who said: love — will stun the life out of you!

"This is life — on the rails! Don't cry!"

Rights of way — easements — rights of way . . .
(Owners reluctant to look into the eyes
Of their horses bound for slaughter).

"Unbroken and seamless, there is
No such happiness. Did I really buy it *like that*?"
The dressmaker was right, who held
Her tongue about it: "Use cross-ties."

24 September 1923

THE PRAGUE KNIGHT

Blanch—faced
Guardian of the age-old lapping —
Knight, knight,
Keeping watch on the river.

(O could I find peace
In it from arms and mouths?!)
Sen—ti—nel
Set at your post of partings.

The oaths, the rings . . .
Yes, like stones into the river
How many — of us
Over four centuries!

Admission into the waters
Is free. As are roses — in bloom!
He's thrown me over — I'll throw myself over!
That's vengeance for you!

We never tire of this
— So long as passion exists!
Taking our vengeance off bridges.
Making short but wide work of us,

My wings! Into the slime,
Into the scum — like brocade!

No lament for the moment
Over the bridge—toll!

— "Off a fatal bridge
Down — I dare myself!"
I, at a level with you,
Prague Knight.

Whether it's sweetness or sadness
In it — is clearer to you,
Knight, watching over
The river — of days.

27 September 1923

ПРАЖСКИЙ РЫЦАРЬ

Бледно — лицый
Страж над плеском века —
Рыцарь, рыцарь,
Стерегущий реку.

(О найду ль в ней
Мир от губ и рук?!)
Ка — ра — ульный
На посту разлук.

Клятвы, кольца . . .
Да, но камнем в реку
Нас-то — сколько
За четыре века!

В воду пропуск
Вольный. Розам — цвесть!
Бросил — брошусь!
Вот тебе и месть!

Не устанем
Мы — доколе страсть есть!
Мстить мостами.
Широко расправьтесь,

Крылья! В тину,
В пену — как в парчу!

Мосто — вины
Нынче не плачу!

— «С рокового мосту
Вниз — отважься!»
Я тебе по росту,
Рыцарь пражский.

Сласть ли, грусть ли
В ней — тебе видней,
Рыцарь, стерегущий
Реку — дней.

27 сентября 1923

NIGHT PLACES

The darkest of nights'
Places: a bridge. — Lips to lips!
Really should we be lugging
Our shared cross to these unholy places,

There: into the dancing gaslight
Of eyes, of gauze . . . Into a rented Sodom?
Onto a cot, where everyone has been!
Onto a cot, where no one

Goes alone . . . The lamp goes out.
Perhaps — conscience will sleep!
(The most faithful of nights'
Places — is death!) The rented narrowness

Of night — water has greater largesse!
Water — smoother than sheets!
Love — caprice and calamity!
There — into deep cold blue!

If only we were fit for the beliefs
Of the age! Having locked arms!
(The river — goes easy on a body,
And sleep — beats living!)

Love: chill to the bone!
Love: white-hot heat!
Water — loves endings.
The river — loves bodies.

4 October 1923

НОЧНЫЕ МЕСТА

Темнейшее из ночных
Мест: мост. — Устами в уста!
Неужели ж нам свой крест
Тащить в дурные места,

Туда: в веселящий газ
Глаз, газа . . . В платный Содом?
На койку, где все до нас!
На койку, где не вдвоем

Никто . . . Никнет ночник.
Авось — совесть уснет!
(Вернейшее из ночных
Мест — смерть!) Платных теснот

Ночных — блаже вода!
Вода — глаже простынь!
Любить — блажь и беда!
Туда — в хладную синь!

Когда б в веры века
Нам встать! Руки смежив!
(Река — телу легка,
И спать — лучше, чем жить!)

Любовь: зноб до кости!
Любовь: зной до бела!
Вода — любит концы.
Река — любит тела.

4 октября 1923

A GIRLFRIEND

"I'm not leaving! — This isn't the end!" And she clings, and clings . . .
But in her breast — the swell
Of looming waters,
Of notes . . . Count on it: sealed as
A sacrament: we're bound — to leave each other!

5 October 1923

ПОДРУГА (1923 Г)

«Не расстанусь! — Конца нет!» И льнет, и льнет . . .
А в груди — нарастание
Грозных вод,
Нот . . . Надёжное: как таинство
Непреложное: рас — станемся!

5 октября 1923

LIFE TRAIN

If not a bayonet — then a tusk, a snowbank, a squall, —
On the hour, another train — to Immortality!
I came and knew one thing: it's just another stop.
And not worth unpacking.

Upon everyone, everything — my indifferent eyes,
Come to rest — on the immemorial.
O how natural to enter third class
Through the closeness of the ladies' rooms!

Where after warmed-over cutlets, cheeks
Are grown cold . . . — Can't we go further,
My soul? I'd sooner go down a streetlamp's drain
To escape this deadening discord:

Of end papers, diapers,
Red-hot curling irons,
Scorched hair,
Women's hats, oil cloths,
All the eau-de-Col—ognes
Of families, the joys
Of sewing (Mere trifles!)
Is there a coffeepot?
Crackers, pillows, matrons, nannies,
The closeness of nurseries, and baths.

I don't want to be in this box of women's bodies
Waiting on the hour of my death!

I want this train to be drinking and singing:
Death — too, belongs in another class!

In a daze, a stupor, on a concertina, in distress, in vanity!
— These unbelievers do cling *so* to life! —
Prompting some pilgrim or other to say: *"In the next world"* . . .
So I interrupt to say: it must be better!

A platform. — And sleepers. — And a last shrub
In my hand — I let loose. — It's too late
To hang on. — Sleepers. — I'm tired
Of so many mouths. — I look to the stars.

So through a rainbow of all the vanishing
Planets — did someone at least number them? —
I look and see one thing: another end.
And not worth regretting.

6 October 1923

ПОЕЗД ЖИЗНИ

Не штык — так клык, так сугроб, так шквал, —
В Бессмертье что час — то поезд!
Пришла и знала одно: вокзал.
Раскладываться не стоит.

На всех, на всё — равнодушьем глаз,
Которым конец — исконность.
О как естественно в третий класс
Из душности дамских комнат!

Где от котлет разогретых, щек
Остывших . . . — Нельзя ли дальше,
Душа? Хотя бы в фонарный сток
От этой фатальной фальши:

Папильоток, пеленок,
Щипцов каленых,
Волос паленых,
Чепцов, клеенок,
О — де — ко — лонов
Семейных, швейных
Счастий (klein wenig!)*
Взят ли кофейник?
Сушек, подушек, матрон, нянь,
Душности бонн, бань.

Не хочу в этом коробе женских тел

Ждать смертного часа!
Я хочу, чтобы поезд и пил и пел:
Смерть — тоже вне класса!

В удаль, в одурь, в гармошку, в надсад, в тщету!
— Эти нехристи и льнут же! —
Чтоб какой-нибудь странник: «На тем свету» . . .
Не дождавшись скажу: лучше!

Площадка. — И шпалы. — И крайний куст
В руке. — Отпускаю. — Поздно
Держаться. — Шпалы. — От стольких уст
Устала. — Гляжу на звезды.

Так через радугу всех планет
Пропавших — считал-то кто их? —
Гляжу и вижу одно: конец.
Раскаиваться не стоит.

6 октября 1923

* * *

An ancient vanity runs in my veins,
An ancient dream: to go with my beloved!

To the River Nile! (Not to lie on his breast, but to enter it!)
To the River Nile — or just anywhere

Farther on! Beyond the limiting limits
Of these stops! You understand, that I want

Out — of this body! (The hour our eyelids close
Will we really step out — of these garments?)

. . . Beyond the boundaries of the other world:
To the River Styx! . .

7 October 1923

ДРЕВНЯЯ ТЩЕТА ТЕЧЕТ ПО ЖИЛАМ . . .

Древняя тщета течет по жилам,
Древняя мечта: уехать с милым!

К Нилу! (Не на грудь хотим, а в грудь!)
К Нилу — иль еще куда-нибудь

Дальше! За предельные пределы
Станций! Понимаешь, что из тела

Вон — хочу! (В час тупящихся вежд
Разве выступаем — из одежд?)

. . . За потустороннюю границу:
К Стиксу!..

7 октября 1923

ESCAPE

Hidden under a curtain of rain
From more indifferent eyes,
— O, my future! — for you
I watch — like a bomber

Watching and waiting for a train
With his still-shattering explosion
In hand . . . (We don't just flee
Murderers, ducking into falling

Rain!) Fearless of punishment,
No . . . — But of clouds? of bells!
This is the Future full steam ahead
Rushing past a platform

That vanishes . . . God! Good!
God! And into covering smoke —
Like a standing wall . . . (Underfoot
A running board — or are our legs,

And arms already gone?) Mile markers
On poles . . . Lanterns out of fog . . .
O no, it's not love, or passion,
Escape, you are the train I ride

Into Immortality . . .

14 October 1923

ПОБЕГ

Под занавесом дождя
От глаз равнодушных кроясь,
— О завтра мое! — тебя
Выглядываю — как поезд

Выглядывает бомбист
С еще-сотрясеньем взрыва
В руке . . . (Не одних убийств
Бежим, зарываясь в гриву

Дождя!) Не расправы страх,
Не . . . — Но облака! но звоны!
То Завтра на всех парах
Проносится вдоль перрона

Пропавшего . . . Бог! Благой!
Бог! И в дымовую опушь —
Как об стену . . . (Под ногой
Подножка — или ни ног уж,

Ни рук?) Верстовая снасть
Столба . . . Фонари из бреда . . .
О нет, не любовь, не страсть,
Ты поезд, которым еду

В Бессмертье . . .

14 октября 1923

* * *

I wander — not one to build a home,
Having settled at a cross-roads!
So, in spite of the expanse
Of space, accursed bed-sheets

Of parting, with a passing favorite
Stealing off into the night's mystery,
It's you under every rusted
Corbel of the streetlamps —

With the edge of your cloak . . . Beyond a grill —
With the edge of glass . . . (Still a tiny edge
Of glass!) Insistent corpse,
Why do you swing — before my eyes?

Along embankments — shivering oaths,
Along fences — collapsing rhymes.
Embracing — "I'll hold you more passionately",
Listening — "I'll listen to you more attentively".

Always and only you, in every place,
In every color, on every bridge.
With my sighs — as their rigging!
With my oaths — as their paving stones!

Such power does the lyre of a lover
Have over the contradictions of time,
That it's to you, who have not been mine,
I look back — to see some glimpse of my future!

16 October 1923

* * *

I love — but the pain lives on.
Find me soothing words:

Rainy ones, — as might be wasted by anyone
Making up his own, until in these leaves

The rain is audible: not a flail on a sheaf:
Rain beats on the roof: on my forehead,

On my coffin, until it dawns — on me,
My shivering — has stopped, until one has slept

And slept . . .
                    It's through the chinks, they say,
Water escapes. Others may lie
In file, uncomplaining, waiting
The unknown. (Me — they can burn).

Soothe me — and I ask, be a friend:
Not with letters, but the small room of your arms:

With comforts . . .

24 October 1923

POEM OF THE HILL

Love, do my words
startle you? Parting makes us
all talk like drunks
and love solemnity . . .
                    Hölderlin

DEDICATION

You shrug — the load slips off your shoulders;
Your soul — soars.
But I will sing about sorrow:
About my hill!

Not today, nor even tomorrow shall I be able
To fill its caldera.
And I will sing about sorrow
At the top of my hill.

1

My hill was the body of a recruit
Brought down by a shell.
My hill wanted the lips
Of a virgin, my hill

Expected nuptials.
— An ocean in the ear's helix,
A sudden-bursting hurrah! —
My hill strove and stood ground.

My hill was thunder! My breast,
A prize Titans advanced upon!
(The last house on my hill —
Remember — outside town?)

My hill was — worlds!
Now God exacts his price for my world!

. . . .

My sorrow began with my hill.
My hill above town.

2

No Parnassus, no Sinai,
Just my bare, barracks
Hill! — Right face! Fire!
Why, to my eyes, then
(As it was October, not May)
Was my hill — Paradise?

3

Offered on your palm:
Paradise — don't touch it; it's hot!
My hill with its rutted slope
Collapsed beneath our feet.

With the paws of a Titan
With its bushes and conifers —
My hill raked our coats,
Ordering: Halt!

O, far from a veritable
Paradise — blast after blast!
My hill threw us on our backs,
Commanding: Lie there!

Dumbstruck at the onslaught,
— How? To this day, I don't care! —
My hill, my procuress — opened
Its holy relics, pointing: Here . . .

4

Persephone's pomegranate seed,
How can I forget you in these hard winter frosts?
I remember your lips, a warm bi-valve shell
Half-open on my own.

Persephone ruined by a seed!
The stubborn crimson of your lips,
And your eyelashes' separate tips
Enmeshed in the gold, separated tips of a star.

5

Passion — is no trick, and no fiction!
It doesn't lie — just don't try to make it last!
O, if only we had come into this world
As commonplace lovers!

O, if only we had been sensible and unceremonious:
This would be just — my hill; this, simply — my mound . . .
They say — the greater the pull to the edge
The higher the precipice.

In masses of brown heather,
Among islands of weeping conifer . . .
(At the height of delirium —
Above the level of others' humdrum lives)
                              — Take me, then! I'm yours . . .

Lacking the tender mercy of family,
Lacking the prattle of little mouths — we grieve!
That we came into this world
As larger-than-life lovers!

6

My hill grieved (and hills do grieve
With bitter clay at the hour of parting),
My hill grieved for the dove-grey
Tenderness of our undiscovered mornings.

My hill grieved for our companionship:
For the immutable kinship of our lips!
My hill said: from each shall it be rent
According to his *tears*.

And my hill grieved that life is a moveable
Feast, a continual bartering of hearts!
And my hill grieved: if only she were
With child — he could let Hagar go!

And my hill said it was a demon's
Scheme, to toy with us each, in turn.
My hill spoke. We were mute.
We left it to my hill to judge.

7

My hill grieved that only sadness
Would come — of this day's blood and fire.
My hill said it would not let us go,
That it would not let you live with another!

My hill grieved that only smoke
Would come — of this day's Empire and Rome.
My hill said we would live with others
(Not that I envy them, the others!)

My hill grieved for the terrible weight
Of vows too late to be foresworn.
My hill grieved that our knot was ancient —
Gordian: duty and passion.

My hill grieved for our sorrow:
Tomorrow: Not now! When over our heads —
Is no *memento* set, just — this *sea*!
Tomorrow — when we may come to know.

A sound . . . as if someone were just —
Well . . . weeping nearby?
My hill grieved that we must go down
Separately, through such mud —

Back into life, which we all know is:
A rabble — a market — a barracks.
And my hill said — all poems
About hills — are written — *like this.*

8

My hill was the heave
Of Atlas, of a groaning Titan.
My hill will be the pride of a city
Where from morning to night, we've

Played out our lives — trumped, in spades!
Passionate, we try stubbornly *not to be,*
Not to fall to the level of a bearish roar,
Not to rise to the spectacle of the town-clock's twelve apostles —

Honor my dark grotto.
(I was a grotto — and waves leapt into it!)
Our final hand, as we were dealt it —
Remember — outside of town?

My hill was — worlds!
All gods take vengeance on their likenesses!

. . . .

My sorrow began with my hill.
My hill will be — my monument.

9

Years will pass. And lo — the aforesaid
Stone is tamely replaced — with a flat slab.
Over my hill they will build summer cottages,
They will cut it into little fenced lots.

In these outskirts they will claim
The air is better and life easier.
They will begin to cut out their plots
And raise their joists, their timbers,

And straighten out my hilly passages,
All my ravines — filled and leveled!
Because some people at least must have
A home for their happiness, and *happiness* — at home!

Happiness — *at home!* Love without illusion!
Without torment — without fighting!
I must be a woman — and endure!
(Times were, when he came, there

Was happiness — in my home!) Love, unsharpened
By parting or the knife.
On the ruins of our happiness
A city will rise: of husbands and wives.

And in our same blessed air,
–If you can manage it — fuck it!–

Small shopkeepers on holiday
Will eat through their profits,

Laying out floors and passageways,
So long as every line — leads them home!
Because some people at least need
A roof with a stork's nest on it!

10

Still, under the weight of their foundations,
My hill will not forget — our playfulness,
Dissipated, but — unforgotten:
Hills of times — lie buried in my hill!

Walking its persistent gullies
Summer people will learn too late:
This is no little hill, overgrown with families —
This is a crater, in current circulation!

Grapevines won't hold back — Vesuvius!
Flax can't tie down — my Giant!
A *single* mad kiss would be enough —
To set the vineyards stirring with lions

Who will let roar — let vomit
My molten lava of hatred.
Your daughters — each sluts;
And your sons — poets!

Your daughter — lately delivered of a bastard!
Your son — wasted on gypsies!
You will never be led by green pastures,
You, who feed on my blood!

Firmer than a corner-stone,
Than a deathbed vow: I say:

There will be no earthly happiness for you,
You ants, on my hill!

God knows what hour, what day,
You will see, you and all your family,
My inordinate, my huge
Hill is Monument to his Seventh Commandment!

ПОЭМА ГОРЫ

> *Liebster, Dich wundert*
> *die Rede? Alle Scheidenden*
> *reden wie Trunkene und*
> *nehmen gerne sich festlich . . .*
> Holderlin*

ПОСВЯЩЕНИЕ

Вздрогнешь — и горы с плеч,
И душа — горе.
Дай мне о горе спеть:
О моей горе!

Черной ни днесь, ни впредь
Не заткну дыры.
Дай мне о горе спеть
На верху горы.

1

Та гора была, как грудь
Рекрута, снарядом сваленного.
Та гора хотела губ
Девственных, обряда свадебного

Требовала та гора.
— Океан в ушную раковину
Вдруг-ворвавшимся ура!
Та гора гнала и ратовала.

Та гора была, как гром!
Зря с титанами заигрываем!
Той горы последний дом
Помнишь — на исходе пригорода?

Та гора была — миры!
Бог за мир взымает дорого!

. . . .

Горе началось с горы.
Та гора была над городом.

2

Не Парнас, не Синай —
Просто голый казарменный
Холм. — Равняйся! Стреляй!
Отчего же глазам моим
(Раз октябрь, а не май)
Та гора была — рай?

3

Как на ладони поданный
Рай — не берись, коль жгуч!
Гора бросалась под ноги
Колдобинами круч.

Как бы титана лапами
Кустарников и хвой —
Гора хватала за полы,
Приказывала: стой!

О, далеко не азбучный
Рай — сквознякам сквозняк!
Гора валила навзничь нас,
Притягивала: ляг!

Оторопев под натиском,
— Как? Не понять и днесь!
Гора, как сводня — святости,
Указывала: здесь . . .

4

Персефоны зерно гранатовое!
Как забыть тебя в стужах зим?
Помню губы, двойною раковиной
Приоткрывшиеся моим.

Персефона, зерном загубленная!
Губ упорствующий багрец,
И ресницы твои — зазубринами,
И звезды золотой зубец . . .

5

Не обман — страсть, и не вымысел,
И не лжет, — только не дли!
О когда бы в сей мир явились мы
Простолюдинами любви!

О когда б, здраво и попросту:
Просто — холм, просто — бугор . . .
(Говорят — тягою к пропасти
Измеряют уровень гор.)

В ворохах вереска бурого,
В островах страждущих хвой . . .
(Высота бреда — над уровнем
Жизни.)
— На же меня! Твой . . .

Но семьи тихие милости,
Но птенцов лепет — увы!
Оттого что в сей мир явились мы —
Небожителями любви!

6

Гора горевала (а горы глиной
Горькой горюют в часы разлук),
Гора горевала о голубиной
Нежности наших безвестных утр.

Гора горевала о нашей дружбе:
Губ — непреложнейшее родство!
Гора говорила, что коемужды
Сбудется — по слезам его.

Еще говорила гора, что табор —
Жизнь, что весь век по сердцам базарь!
Еще горевала гора: хотя бы
С дитятком — отпустил Агарь!

Еще говорила, что это — демон
Крутит, что замысла нет в игре.
Гора говорила, мы были немы.
Предоставляли судить горе.

7

Гора горевала, что только грустью
Станет — что ныне и кровь и зной.
Гора говорила, что не отпустит
Нас, не допустит тебя с другой!

Гора горевала, что только дымом
Станет — что ныне: и мир, и Рим.
Гора говорила, что быть с другими
Нам (не завидую тем другим!).

Гора горевала о страшном грузе
Клятвы, которую поздно клясть.
Гора говорила, что стар тот узел
Гордиев — долг и страсть.

Гора горевала о нашем горе —
Завтра! Не сразу! Когда над лбом —
Уж не memento**, а просто — море!
Завтра, когда поймем.

Звук . . . Ну как будто бы кто-то просто,
Ну . . . плачет вблизи?
Гора горевала о том, что врозь нам
Вниз, по такой грязи —

В жизнь, про которую знаем все мы:
Сброд — рынок — барак.
Еще говорила, что все поэмы
Гор — пишутся — так.

8

Та гора была, как горб
Атласа, титана стонущего.
Той горою будет горд
Город, где с утра и до ночи мы

Жизнь свою — как карту бьем!
Страстные, не быть упорствуем.
Наравне с медвежьим рвом
И двенадцатью апостолами —

Чтите мой угрюмый грот.
(Грот — была, и волны впрыгивали!)
Той игры последний ход
Помнишь — на исходе пригорода?

Та гора была — миры!
Боги мстят своим подобиям!
. . . .
Горе началось с горы.
Та гора на мне — надгробием.

9

Минут годы, и вот означенный
Камень, плоским смененный, снят***.
Нашу гору застроят дачами, —
Палисадниками стеснят.

Говорят, на таких окраинах
Воздух чище и легче жить.
И пойдут лоскуты выкраивать,
Перекладинами рябить.

Перевалы мои выструнивать,
Все овраги мои вверх дном!
Ибо надо ведь — хоть кому-нибудь
Дома — в счастье, и счастья в дом!

Счастья — в доме! Любви без вымыслов!
Без вытягивания жил!
Надо женщиной быть — и вынести!
(Было-было, когда ходил,

Счастье — в доме!) Любви, не скрашенной
Ни разлукою, ни ножом.
На развалинах счастья нашего
Город встанет — мужей и жен.

И на том же блаженном воздухе,
— Пока можешь еще — греши! —

Будут лавочники на отдыхе
Пережевывать барыши,

Этажи и ходы надумывать,
Чтобы каждая нитка — в дом!
Ибо надо ведь — хоть кому-нибудь
Крыши с аистовым гнездом!

10

Но под тяжестью тех фундаментов
Не забудет гора — игры.
Есть беспутные, нет беспамятных:
Горы времени — у горы!

По упорствующим расселинам
Дачник, поздно хватясь, поймет:
Не пригорок, поросший семьями, —
Кратер, пущенный в оборот!

Виноградниками Везувия
Не сковать! Великана льном
Не связать! Одного безумия
Уст — достаточно, чтобы львом

Виноградники заворочались,
Лаву ненависти струя.
Будут девками ваши дочери
И поэтами — сыновья!

Дочь, ребенка расти внебрачного!
Сын, цыганкам себя страви!
Да не будет вам места злачного,
Телеса, на моей крови!

Тверже камня краеугольного,
Клятвой смертника на одре:

— Да не будет вам счастья дольнего,
Муравьи, на моей горе!

В час неведомый, в срок негаданный
Опознаете всей семьей
Непомерную и громадную
Гору заповеди седьмой!

ПОСЛЕСЛОВИЕ

Есть пробелы в памяти, бельма
На глазах: семь покрывал . . .
Я не помню тебя — отдельно.
Вместо черт — белый провал.

Без примет. Белым пробелом —
Весь. (Душа, в ранах сплошных,
Рана — сплошь.) Частности мелом
Отмечать — дело портных.

Небосвод — цельным основан.
Океан — скопище брызг?!
Без примет. Верно — особый —
Весь. Любовь — связь, а не сыск.

Вороной, русой ли масти —
Пусть сосед скажет: он зряч.
Разве страсть — делит на части?
Часовщик я, или врач?

Ты — как круг, полный и цельный:
Цельный вихрь, полный столбняк.
Я не помню тебя отдельно
От любви. Равенства знак.

(В ворохах сонного пуха:
Водопад, пены холмы —

379

Новизной, странной для слуха,
Вместо: я — тронное: мы . . .)

Но зато, в нищей и тесной
Жизни — «жизнь, как она есть» —
Я не вижу тебя совместно
Ни с одной:
— Памяти месть.

1 января — I февраля 1924
Прага. Гора.
Декабрь 1939. Голицыно, Дом писателей

---

* О любимый! Тебя удивляет эта речь? Все расстающиеся говорят как пьяные и любят торжественность . . . Гёльдерлин (пер. М. Цветаевой).

** Memento mori (лат.) — помни о смерти.

*** Т. е. вместо этого камня (горы на мне) будет плоский (плита) (прим. М. Цветаевой).

AFTERWORD

Gaps in my memory — cataracts
In my eyes: back of seven veils.
I fail to recall any detail of you.
A white blank – where your features were.

Unmarked. You as a whole — a white
Gap. (My soul — is one unbroken
Wound.) To chalk-mark the least detail
Would be – the poor work of a tailor.

Our firmament — with its solid feet.
Our ocean — its assemblage of spray?!
Unmarked. Likely — you were unique —
On the whole. Love — a connection, not an investigation.

Black hair, possibly auburn —
Let the curious neighbor say: he could see.
Is it passion's work — to take people apart?
Am I your watchmaker, your surgeon?

You: a circle: complete and entire:
Entire whirlwind, *complete* stupor.
I can't recall you apart
From love. There's an equivalent.

(Over my bed's mass of sleepy down:
My waterfall, its hills of foam —

This is new, strange to my ear,
Instead of: — I your royal: *We are . . .*)

And still, in my poor, constricted
Life: "in my life as it is" —
I can't see you with a single, solitary
Other woman: this

        –is the vengeance of memory!

> *January 1-February 1, 1924*
> *Prague. The Hill.*

POEM OF THE END

1

In the sky, rustier than tin,
A finger, a pole.
Risen in our appointed place,
Like fate.

— Quarter to. Right?
— Death wouldn't have waited.
Smooth. Exaggerated.
He tosses his hat.

In every eyelash — challenge.
His mouth — clenched.
Low. Exaggerated.
He bows to me.

— Quarter to. Sharp? —
His voice rings false.
My heart sinks: what's wrong?
Brain speaks: watch out!

———————————

Sky of ugly portents:
Rust and tin.

He's waited at our usual place.
It's six.

Our kiss is soundless:
Stuporous lips.
As — one might kiss the hand
Of a queen or — corpse . . .

Some hurrying idiot
Shoves an elbow — into my side.
Boring. Exaggerated.
Some siren begins to wail.

And wails, — like a howling dog,
Long-drawn, raging.
(The exaggeration of life
At the point of death.)

What yesterday — rose to my waist
Is risen — beyond the stars.
(Is exaggerated, that is:
At flood-stage).

To myself: darling, darling.
— What time is it? Past six.
To the cinema, or . . . —
His explosion: Home!

2

Wandering tribe, —
See where this brought us!
Thunder over our heads,
A drawn sword,

All the ghastly
Words, lying in ambush,
Like a house collapsing —
One word: Home.

———————————

Wail of a lost, spoilt
Child: home!
A one-year-old's grunting;
"Give me" and "mine"!

My friend in dissipation,
My chill and fever,
Much as others long to stray,
You want — to go there!

———————————

Like a horse, jerking its tether —
Up! — so the rope breaks.

— There's no house, is there?!
— There is, — ten steps more:

A house on the hill. — Any higher?
— A house on top of the hill.
A window set under the eaves.
— *"Lit, and not by a single morning's*

Sun?" Then, back to life, again?
— That would be the simplicity of poetry!
House, that means: out-of-the-house
Into the night.

               (O, to whom shall I breathe

My sorrow, my misfortune,
My terror, greener than ice? . . .)
— You've thought too much. —
A thoughtful reply: — Yes.

3

Then — the embankment. I follow
The water's edge, as if it were solid and thick.
Semiramis' hanging gardens —
So this — is where you are!

The water's — a steely strip,
The color of a corpse —
Which I follow, as a singer
Follows her sheet-music, as one blind —

Follows the edge of a wall . . . Come back!?
No? If I crouch — will you listen?
To the quencher of all thirsts
I cling, like a lunatic

To a gutter . . .
           And I'm not shivering
From the river — for I was born Naiad!
To follow the river, as if it were your hand,
Of a lover, walking beside me —

And faithful . . .
           The dead are faithful.
Yes, but not everyone dies in a squalid room . . .
Death to the left, and to the right —
You. My right side numb, as if it were dead.

Shaft of stunning light.
Laugh, like a cheap tambourine.
— You and I need to . . .

                    (Shivering.)

— Will we have the courage?

4

A wave of fair-haired
Mist — a flounce of gauze.
Much too stale, much too smoky,
And, above all — too much talk!
What does it reek of? Extreme haste,
Indulgence and peccadillo:
Inside information
And ballroom powder.

Men with children, acting single,
Wearing their rings, venerable youths . . .
Too many jokes, too much laughter,
And above all — too much calculation!
Prominent and petty, alike,
Top to bottom.
. . . Inside trading
And ballroom powder.

(Half-turned away: is *this* —
Our house? — No, I won't be your hostess!)
One — bending over his checkbook,
Another — over a tiny kidskin glove,
And another — over a little patent leather pump
Works unobtrusively.
. . . Advantageous marriages
And ballroom powder.

Silver notches at the window —
Like a Star of Malta!
Too much caressing, too much petting,
And above all — too much pawing!
Too much pinching . . . (Yesterday's
Leftovers — don't be so picky: they are ripe!)
. . . Commercial intrigues
And ballroom powder.

Do you think this chain's too short?
But then it's not just plated; it's platinum!
With their triple chins
Trembling, they chew — their veal
Like calves. Over each sweet neck
A devil — a gas burner.
. . . Business failures
And some brand of gunpowder —
Bertold Schwartz's . . .

                         He was so
Gifted — such a philanthropist.
— We need to talk.
Will we have the courage?

5

I detect movement in his lips.
But know — he won't speak first.
— You don't love me? — No, I love you.
— You don't love me! — But I'm tormented,

And wasted, and worn out.
(Like an eagle surveying the terrain):
— You call *this* — a home?
— Home is — in my heart. — How very literary!

Love is flesh and blood.
A flower — watered with blood.
Do you think love is —
Idle chat across a table?

An hour — and then we both just go home?
Like these ladies and gentlemen?
Love is . . .
                        — An altar?
Sweetheart, to that altar bring scar

Upon scar! — Under the eyes of waiters
And revelers? (I think:
"Love is — a bow drawn
Taut: a bow: separation").

— Love is — a connection. When
Everything we have is separate: our mouths, our lives.

(I did ask you: not to speak of it!
Our hour that was secret, close,

That hour on top of the hill,
That hour of passion. Memento — like smoke:
Love is — all one's gifts
Into the fire, — and always — for nothing!)

The shell-like slit of your mouth
Goes white. No smile — an inventory.
— First on the list, one
Bed.
      — You may as well have said

One wide gulf? — The drum-wail
Of your fingers. — I'm not asking you to move mountains!
Love means . . .
          — You are mine.
I understand you. So?

————————————

The drum-wail of your fingers
Grows louder. (Scaffold and square.)
— Let's go away. — And I: Let's die,
I was hoping. It would be simpler!

Enough of this squalor:
Rhymes, rails, rooms, stations . . .
— Love is: a life.
— No, it was something else

To the ancients . . .

              — So what? —

                          The shreds

Of a handkerchief in my fist, like a fish.

— So, should we go? — And what would we take?

Prison, the rails, a bullet — you choose!

Death — and none of these arrangements!

— A life! — Like a Roman tribune,

Surveying the remnants of his force

Like an eagle.

                  — Then, we should say goodbye.

6

— I didn't want that.
Not that. (I'm thinking: listen!
Desire is the traffic of bodies,
While we should be souls — to each other

Hereafter . . .) — And he didn't say it.
(Right, when the time comes for the train to pull out,
You let pass to your women, as it were some
Goblet, the sad honor of

Parting . . .) — Perhaps it's my delirium?
Did I hear you right? (You, polite liar,
Letting pass to your lover, as it were some
Bouquet, the blood-stained honor of this

Rupture . . .) — Clearly: syllable
After syllable, so — should say goodbye,
That's what you said? (As it were some handkerchief,
Let drop at a point of sweet

Excess . . .) — In this battle
You — are Caesar. (O, what an impudent thrust!
To let pass to your adversary the sword
You surrender, as if it were a

Trophy!) — He goes on: (some ringing
In my ears . . .) — I double over:

The first time I am spoken of personally
In this break-up. — Do you say this to every woman?

Don't deny it! A vengeance,
Worthy of Lovelace.
A gesture, doing you honor,
And stripping the meat from my

Bones — A chuckle. Above the laughter —
Death. A gesture. (Without desire.
Desire is the traffic — *of others,*
While we shall be shades — to each other

Hereafter . . .) A last nail
Driven home. A screw, if the coffin is lead.
— A last, very last request.
— Yes. — Not a word, ever,

About us . . . to any . . . well . . .
Men after me. (From their stretchers
The wounded — do yearn for spring!)
— And I would ask the same of you.

Should I give you a ring, a keepsake?
— No. — Your wide-open eyes are
Unreadable. (Like a seal
Set upon your heart, a signet ring

On your finger . . . No scenes!
I swallow.) More ingratiatingly, quieter:

— A book then? — What, like you give to everyone?
No, don't even write them, those

Books . . .

——————————————————

This means, I mustn't.
This means, I mustn't.
Mustn't cry.

In our wandering
Fisherman's tribe we
Dance — and don't cry.

Drink — and don't cry.
Pay with our hot
Blood — and don't cry.

Pearls in a glass,
Melt — and rule
The world — and don't cry.

— So it's me who's leaving? — I see
Right through you. Harlequin, for her fidelity,
You fling your own Pierrette — a bone,
That most contemptible

Prize: the honor of ending it,
Of ringing down the curtain. The last

Word. An inch of lead
In my breast: would be better, hotter

And — cleaner . . .

                My teeth
Press into my lips.
I will not cry.

All my strength — to press into
My softest flesh.
And not cry.

In our wandering tribe
We die, and don't cry,
Burn, and don't cry.

In ashes and in songs,
We do bury the dead
In our wandering tribe.

— So am I first? Mine the first move?
As in chess then? And
You see, even mounting a scaffold
Men ask we go first . . .

                      — And quickly.

Then please, don't look! — One glance, —
(Any moment mine will come thick and fast!
And then how will I drive them back
Into my eyes?!) — I tell you, you mustn't

Look!!!

Clearly and abruptly,
Looking up:
— Darling, let's go,
Or I'm going to cry!

———————————

I forgot! Among all the breathing
Moneyboxes (and commodities!)
The blonde back of *her* head flashed:
Wheat, corn, rye!

All the commandments of Sinai
Washed away — Maenads' pelts! —
In a pile to rival Golkonda,
That storehouse of pleasure —

(For everyone!) Nature doesn't amass
Riches in vain, is not completely niggard!
From these blonde tropics, my
Hunter, — how will you find your way

Back? With her rude nakedness,
Teasing and dazzling to tears —
Adultery, like solid gold,
Pours out. Laughing.

— Isn't it true? — A clinging, pushy
Look. In every eyelash — an urge.

— And above all — at her core!
A gesture that twists into a braid.

O, gesture that is already tearing off —
Its clothing! Easier than eating or drinking —
A smile! (For you, there's some hope,
Alas, of salvation!)

From — that nurse or your fraternal order?
From an ally: from our alliance!
— Buried as I am — to be able to laugh!
(And unburied — I laugh.)

7

Then — the embankment. A last.
That's all. Apart, not holding hands,
Like neighbors avoiding each other,
We wander on. Away from the riverside —

Weeping. Salty, falling
Quicksilver I lick away, not caring:
Whether Heaven sent Great Solomon's
Moon to meet my tears.

A pole. Why not bang my forehead against it
Until it bleeds? Until it shatters, not just until it bleeds!
Like two criminal accomplices, fearful,
We wander on. (What was murdered — is Love.)

Wait! Are these really two lovers? Walking
Into the night? Separately? To sleep with others?
— You understand, the future
Lies there? — I left my head up and back.

— To sleep! — Like newlyweds, on a floor . . .
— To sleep! — When we can't even manage to fall
In step. In time. Plaintively: — Take my arm!
We're not criminals that we have to walk like this! . . .

Electric. (As if it were his *soul* — has
Come to lie! — On my hand.) A current

Strikes through feverish leads and
Excites, — his hand comes to lie on my soul!

And clings. Everything is iridescent! What could be
More iridescent than tears? Like curtains, a rain
Of many beads. — I don't know any banks like this
That really come to an end. — There's a bridge, and:

                                                                    — What then?

Here? (A hearse draws up).
Ca — lm eyes
Fly up. — May I take you home?
A la—st time!

8

A la—st bridge.
(I won't let go, won't pull away!)
A last bridge,
A last toll.

Wa—ter and dry land.
I lay out my coins.
Mo—ney for death,
Charon's token to cross Lethe.

A sha—dow of a coin
Into the hands of a shade. This money
Is sou—ndless.
So, into the hands of a shade —

A sha—dow of a coin.
Without glint, without tinkle.
My coins go—into his.
The dead have their poppies.

A bridge.

Ha—ppy destination
Of lovers without hope:

Bridge, you — are passion:
A convention: an unbroken between.

I nestle: it's warm,
I'm your rib — so I cling.
Neither *ahead of*, nor *behind* you:
At some interval of insight!

Without hands, or feet.
With all my bones and forces:
Only my side is alive, O
Which I press to you, next to me.

The whole of my life — in that side!
Which is — my ear — and my echo.
As the yolk to the white
I cling, like a Samoyed to his fur

I press myself, I cling,
I nestle. Siamese twins,
What are you — to our conjunction?
The woman — you remember: the one you called

Mama? forgetting everything and even
Herself, in the motionless triumph
Of ca—rrying you,
She held you no closer than I do.

See! We like this!
It's true! On your chest you cradled me!

I won't jump do—wn!
To dive — I would have to let go of —

Your hand. I press close,
Press closer . . . And I can't be torn away.
Bridge, you are a bad husband:
A lover — slipping away!

Bridge, you have taken our side!
We feed your river with bodies!
I have fa—stened on you like ivy,
Like a tick: so tear me out by my roots!

Like ivy! Like a tick!
Godless! Inhuman!
To ca—st me aside, like a thing,
Me, who never cared for

A single thing in this
Inflated, material world!
Tell me, it's unreal!
That night follows night — some

Morning, an Ex—press to Rome!
Grenada? Even I don't know,
Throwing back the featherbeds
Of Mont Blancs and Himalayas.

The de—ep valley of the bed:
I warm it with the last of my blood.

Lis—ten to my side!
After all, it's much finer

Than po—etry . . . It's good and warm
Still? Who will you sleep with tomorrow?
Te—ll me it's my imagination!
That there's not, never will be any end

To this bri—dge . . .
                              — As it ends.

———————————————

— Here? — With a child's, or a god's
Gesture. — We—ll? I cling.
— Ju—st once more:
A last time!

9

Walking the factory blocks, loud
And resonant to our call . . .
A concealed, sublingual
Secret of wives from husbands, of widows

From their friends — to you, I impart the whole secret
Eve took from the tree — here:
I am no more than an animal,
Wounded in the belly by someone.

I burn . . . As if it were my soul peeled away with my
Skin! Steam disappeared down a hole,
That notorious and foolish heresy,
We call the soul.

Pallid green Christian sickness!
Steam! You don't treat a soul with poultices!
When it never existed!
There was only a body, who wanted to live,

That now does not want to live.

———————————————

Forgive me! I didn't mean it!
Just a wail out of my gut!

As the condemned await execution
After three in the morning

Over their chessboard . . . Grinning
To mock their warder's eye.
After all, we're just pawns!
And someone plays with all of us.

Who? The kind gods? Or the evil?
In the eye of the peephole —
An eye. Clanging down the red
Corridor. A latch thrown up.

A drag on cheap tobacco.
Spit, we've lived our lives, you know, spit.
. . . These checkered pavements are
A direct route: to the ditch

And to blood. The secret eye:
The moon's hearing eye . . .

. . . .

And casting one sidelong glance:
— How far away you already lie!

10

One mutual
Wince — Our café!

Our island, our chapel,
Where in the mornings we —

Lowlives! Transitory couple! —
Celebrated our matins.

Smell of the market, of something gone sour,
Of drowsiness, of spring . . .
Here the coffee was vile, —
Like burnt oats!

(The spirit of good horses
Is broken with oats!)
Not a bit Arabian —
That coffee stank of

Arcadia . . .

But how she smiled on us,
Sitting us down beside her,
Worldly and compassionate, —
As a grey-haired mistress

With her doting smile:
Carpe diem! Carpe . . . Smiling

On our madness, our poverty,
Our yawning and love, —

And, above all, upon — our youth!
Our giggling — without provocation,
Our laughter — without malice,
Our faces — without lines, —

O, above all, upon — our youth!
Our passions unfit for this climate!
Blown in from somewhere,
Surged in from somewhere

Into this lackluster café:
— Burnous and Tunis! —
On our hopes and our muscles
Under our threadbare robes . . .

(My dear, I'm not complaining:
Scar upon scar!)
O, how she saw us off, our
Proprietress in her stiff cap

Of Dutch linen . . .

———————————

Not quite remembering, not quite understanding,
As if led away from a festival . . .
— Our street! — No longer ours . . . —

— How many times we walked it . . . — but no longer we . . . —

— Tomorrow let the sun rise in the West!
— David break with Jehovah!
— What are we doing? — Separating.
— A word that has no meaning to me,

A supremely senseless word:
— Sep—arating. — Am I just one of a hundred?
Just some word of four syllables,
Beyond which emptiness lies.

Stop! In Serbian, in Croatian,
Really, is it just the Bohemian cropping up in us?
Sep—arating. To separate . . .
A supremely supernatural Babel!

A sound to burst the eardrums,
To test the limits of anguish . . .
Separation — is not a Russian word!
Or a woman's! Or a man's!

Or a god's word! What are we — sheep
To gape as we eat?
Separation — what language is that?
There's no meaning in it,

No sound of it! Well, maybe an empty
Noise — a saw perhaps, through drowsiness.
Separation — is just Khlebnikov's school

Of nightingales groaning,

Of swans . . .

          How did it come to this?
A dammed-up lake gone dry —
Air! The sound of hand clapping hand.
Separation — it's thunder

Over my head . . . An ocean flooding our cabin!
Off our most distant promontory, off our farthest cape!
These streets — are too steep:
To separate — after all, means to descend,

Down the hill . . . Two leaden feet,
A sigh . . . A palm, finally, and a nail!
An overwhelming argument:
To separate — is to go separately,

We — who have grown together . . .

11

To lose everything at a stroke —
Nothing is cleaner!
Beyond town, the outskirts:
An end to our days.

To our legs (read — to stones),
To our days, our homes, and to us.

Abandoned summer homes! Like mothers
Grown old — just so, do I revere them.
It is, after all, something — to stand vacant:
Nothing hollow can stand vacant.

(Summer-homes, standing half-vacant,
Better you were to burn down!)

Just don't cringe,
Re-opening the wound.
Beyond town, beyond town,
Breaking the sutures!

For — with no superfluous words,
No magnificent word — love is a line of sutures.

Sutures, and not a sling, sutures — and not a shield.
— O, don't beg me for protection! —

Sutures, with which the dead are sewn in for burial,
With which I am sewn to you.

(Time will tell how strong a seam:
Single or triple stitched!)

One way or another, my friend, — our seams
Would go! To shreds and tatters!
Our only glory is the seam burst open:
By itself, didn't just unravel!

Under the basting — living tissue,
Red, and not rotted!

O, he loses nothing —
Who bursts a seam!
Beyond town, the outskirts:
Our foreheads separate.

On the outskirts they are executing people
Today — wind blowing through brain matter!

O, he loses nothing who departs —
At an hour when dawn catches fire.
I've sewn a whole life for you through the night,
A fair copy, with no loose ends.

So don't upbraid me now, if it's crooked.
The outskirts: stitches ripped out.

Untidy souls —
Marked by scars! . . .
Beyond town, the outskirts . . .
The ravine with its descending sweep

Of outskirts. With the boot of fate,
Hear it — across the watery clay?
. . . Consider my quick hand,
My friend, and the living thread.

The live, clinging thread — no matter how you pick at it!
The la—st lamppost!

———————————————

Here? A conspiratorial —
Look. The lowest form of human —
Look. — Shall we go back up the hill?
A la—st time!

12

Like a heavy mane
Across our eyes: rain. — Hills.
We've passed the outskirts.
We are beyond town.

This place — doesn't belong to us!
Any more than a stepmother — is a mother!
No further. Here
We will lie down and die.

A field. A fence.
As brother and sister.
A life — in the outskirts. —
Build here, beyond town!

Ahh, it's a played-out
Business, gentlemen!
Everywhere — outskirts!
Where are the villages?!

Let the rain tear and rage.
We stand and part.
These three months,
First time we are two!

Did God seek a loan
Of Job, as well?
This isn't working out:
We're beyond town now!

Beyond town! Do you get it? Out of it!
Outside! We've crossed a divide!
Life — is a place no one can live:
A Jew—ish ghetto — . . .

Wouldn't it be a hundred times more
Worthy to be a Wandering Jew?
Since for anyone, who is not vile,
Life is a Jew—ish pogrom —

A life. Only converts survive!
Judases of every faith!
On to the leper colonies!
On to hell! — beyond the Pale! — not back into

Life, — where only converts survive, only
Sheep — go to slaughter!
Underfoot, I trample
My perm—it to live here!

Into the ground! My revenge, on David's
Shield! — Joining the heaps of bodies!
Isn't it fascinating the Jew
Had no wish — to live?!

Ghetto of God's chosen! A divide
And a ditch. Ex—pect no mercy!
In this most Christian of worlds
All poets — are Jews!

13

Knives sharpened on stone,
Sawdust swept
By a broom. Under my hands
It is furry, and wet.

Where are you, twin male
Virtues: hardness, and dryness?
Under my palm —
Tears, and not rain!

O what greater temptation — is there?
Than to make land — turn to water!
When your hard and glittering eyes
Stream under my palm, —

There's no greater loss
For me. An end to the end!
I stroke — I stroke —
I stroke your face.

Such is the arrogance of Marinas
Like me, — of we Polishwomen.
After your eagle eyes
Stream under my palm . . .

You're crying? My friend!
Now I have it all! Forgive me!

O, how big and salty
In my cupped hand!

A man's tears are brutal:
Like an ax striking a forehead!
Cry, with someone later you will
Make up for the shame lost on me.

Out of — the same sea —
We are fish! A flourish:
. . . Like an empty shell
Lips upon lips.

———————————

In your tears
I taste —
Wormwood.
— And tomorrow,
When
I wake up?

14

Down our steep path —
Downhill. The noises of town.
We meet three streetwalkers.
Laughing. At your tears,

Laughing, — both high and
Low, billowing!
Laughing!
            — at your inappropriate,
Shameful, male

Tears, visible
Through the rain — like two scars!
Like a pearl — shameful
On the bronze of a warrior.

Your first tears, and
Your last — o, let them fall! —
Your tears — are pearls
In my crown!

I don't avert my eyes.
I stare — through the downpour.
Go on, you toys of Venus,
Stare! This union of ours

Is more than your attraction,

Your going to bed.
The very Song of Solomon
Gives way to us,

Infamous birds that we are,
Solomon yields to us,
— crying together is better
Than — fooling ourselves!

—————————————

So, into the hollow waves
Of darkness — stooping and equal —
Traceless — and speechless — we
Go down, like a sinking ship.

Prague. 1 February—Illovishchi, 8 June, 1924.

ПОЭМА КОНЦА

1

В небе, ржавее жести,
Перст столба.
Встал на означенном месте,
Как судьба.

— Без четверти. Исправен?
— Смерть не ждет.
Преувеличенно-плавен
Шляпы взлет.

В каждой реснице — вызов.
Рот сведен.
Преувеличенно-низок
Был поклон.

— Без четверти. Точен? —
Голос лгал.
Сердце упало: что с ним?
Мозг: сигнал!

————————————————

Небо дурных предвестий:
Ржавь и жесть.
Ждал на обычном месте.
Время: шесть.

Сей поцелуй без звука:
Губ столбняк.
Так — государыням руку,
Мертвым — так . . .

Мчащийся простолюдин
Локтем — в бок.
Преувеличенно-нуден
Взвыл гудок.

Взвыл, — как собака, взвизгнул,
Длился, злясь.
(Преувеличенность жизни
В смертный час.)

То, что вчера — по пояс,
Вдруг — до звезд.
(Преувеличенно, то есть:
Во весь рост.)

Мысленно: милый, милый.
— Час? Седьмой.
В кинематограф, или?.. —
Взрыв — Домой!

2

Братство таборное, —
Вот куда вело!
Громом на голову,
Саблей наголо,

Всеми ужасами
Слов, которых ждем,
Домом рушащимся —
Слово: дом.

————————————————

Заблудшего баловня
Вопль: домой!
Дитя годовалое:
«Дай» и «мой»!

Мой брат по беспутству,
Мой зноб и зной,
Так из дому рвутся,
Как ты — домой!

————————————————

Конем, рванувшим коновязь —
Ввысь! — и веревка в прах.
— Но никакого дома ведь!
— Есть, — в десяти шагах:

Дом на горе. — Не выше ли?
— Дом на верху горы.
Окно под самой крышею.
— «Не от одной зари

Горящее?» Так сызнова
Жизнь? — Простота поэм!
Дом, это значит: из дому
В ночь.
            (О, кому повем

Печаль мою, беду мою,
Жуть, зеленее льда?..)
— Вы слишком много думали. —
Задумчивое: — Да.

3

И — набережная. Воды
Держусь, как толщи плотной.
Семирамидины сады
Висячие — так вот вы!

Воды (стальная полоса
Мертвецкого оттенка)
Держусь, как нотного листка —
Певица, края стенки —

Слепец . . . Обратно не отдашь?
Нет? Наклонюсь — услышишь?
Всеутолительницы жажд
Держусь, как края крыши

Лунатик . . .
　　　　　　Но не от реки
Дрожь, — рождена наядой!
Реки держаться, как руки,
Когда любимый рядом —

И верен . . .
　　　　　　Мертвые верны.
Да, но не всем в каморке . . .
Смерть с левой, с правой стороны —
Ты. Правый бок как мертвый.

Разительного света сноп.

Смех, как грошовый бубен.

— Нам с вами нужно бы . . .

(Озноб)

— Мы мужественны будем?

4

Тумана белокурого
Волна — воланом газовым.
Надышано, накурено,
А главное — насказано!
Чем пахнет? Спешкой крайнею,
Потачкой и грешком:
Коммерческими тайнами
И бальным порошком.

Холостяки семейные
В перстнях, юнцы маститые . . .
Нашучено, насмеяно,
А главное — насчитано!
И крупными, и мелкими,
И рыльцем, и пушком.
. . . Коммерческими сделками
И бальным порошком.

(Вполоборота: это вот —
Наш дом? — Не я хозяйкою!)
Один — над книжкой чековой,
Другой — над ручкой лайковой,
А тот — над ножкой лаковой
Работает тишком.
. . . Коммерческими браками
И бальным порошком.

Серебряной зазубриной
В окне — звезда мальтийская!
Наласкано, налюблено,
А главное — натискано!
Нащипано . . . (Вчерашняя
Снедь — не взыщи: с душком!)
. . . Коммерческими шашнями
И бальным порошком.

Цепь чересчур короткая?
Зато не сталь, а платина!
Тройными подбородками
Тряся, тельцы — телятину
Жуют. Над шейкой сахарной
Черт — газовым рожком.
. . . Коммерческими крахами
И неким порошком —
Бертольда Шварца . . .

                    Даровит
Был — и заступник людям.
— Нам с вами нужно говорить.
Мы мужественны будем?

5

Движение губ ловлю.
И знаю — не скажет первым.
— Не любите? — Нет, люблю.
— Не любите! — Но истерзан,

Но выпит, но изведен.
(Орлом озирая местность):
— Помилуйте, это — дом?
— Дом — в сердце моем. — Словесность!

Любовь — это плоть и кровь.
Цвет, собственной кровью полит.
Вы думаете, любовь —
Беседовать через столик?

Часочек — и по домам?
Как те господа и дамы?
Любовь, это значит . . .
                                    — Храм?
Дитя, замените шрамом

На шраме! — Под взглядом слуг
И бражников? (Я, без звука:
«Любовь — это значит лук
Натянутый — лук: разлука».)

— Любовь, это значит — связь.
Всё врозь у нас: рты и жизни.

(Просила ж тебя: не сглазь!
В тот час, в сокровенный, ближний,

Тот час на верху горы
И страсти. Memento* — паром:
Любовь — это все дары
В костер, — и всегда — задаром!)

Рта раковинная щель
Бледна. Не усмешка — опись.
— И прежде всего одна
Постель.

      — Вы хотели: пропасть

Сказать? — Барабанный бой
Перстов. — Не горами двигать!
Любовь, это значит . . .

                — Мой.
Я вас понимаю. Вывод?

_____

Перстов барабанный бой
Растет. (Эшафот и площадь.)
— Уедем. — А я: умрем,
Надеялась. Это проще!

Достаточно дешевизн:
Рифм, рельс, номеров, вокзалов . . .

— Любовь, это значит: жизнь.
— Нет, иначе называлось

У древних . . .
      — Итак? —
          Лоскут
Платка в кулаке, как рыба.
— Так едемте? — Ваш маршрут?
Яд, рельсы, свинец — на выбор!

Смерть — и никаких устройств!
— Жизнь! — Как полководец римский,
Орлом озирая войск
Остаток.
      — Тогда простимся.

6

— Я этого не хотел.
Не этого. (Молча: слушай!
Хотеть — это дело тел,
А мы друг для друга — души

Отныне . . .) — И не сказал.
(Да, в час, когда поезд подан,
Вы женщинам, как бокал,
Печальную честь ухода

Вручаете . . .) — Может, бред?
Ослышался? (Лжец учтивый,
Любовнице как букет.
Кровавую честь разрыва

Вручающий . . .) — Внятно: слог
За слогом, итак — простимся,
Сказали вы? (Как платок,
В час сладостного бесчинства

Уроненный . . .) — Битвы сей
Вы — Цезарь. (О, выпад наглый!
Противнику — как трофей,
Им отданную же шпагу

Вручать!) — Продолжает. (Звон
В ушах . . .) — Преклоняюсь дважды:

Впервые опережен
В разрыве. — Вы это каждой?

Не опровергайте! Месть,
Достойная Ловеласа.
Жест, делающий вам честь,
А мне разводящий мясо

От кости. — Смешок. Сквозь смех —
Смерть. Жест. (Никаких хотений.
Хотеть, это дело — тех,
А мы друг для друга — тени

Отныне . . .) Последний гвоздь
Вбит. Винт, ибо гроб свинцовый.
— Последнейшая из просьб.
— Прошу. — Никогда ни слова

О нас . . . Никому из . . . ну . . .
Последующих. (С носилок
Так раненые — в весну!)
— О том же и вас просила б.

Колечко на память дать?
— Нет. — Взгляд, широко-разверстый,
Отсутствует. (Как печать
На сердце твое, как перстень

На руку твою . . . Без сцен!
Съем.) Вкрадчивее и тише:

— Но книгу тебе? — Как всем?
Нет, вовсе их не пишите,

Книг . . .

_____

Значит, не надо.
Значит, не надо.
Плакать не надо.

В наших бродячих
Братствах рыбачьих
Пляшут — не плачут.

Пьют, а не плачут.
Кровью горячей
Платят — не плачут.

Жемчуг в стакане
Плавят — и миром
Правят — не плачут.

— Так я ухожу? — Насквозь
Гляжу. Арлекин, за верность,
Пьеретте своей — как кость
Презреннейшее из первенств

Бросающий: честь конца,
Жест занавеса. Реченье

Последнее. Дюйм свинца
В грудь: лучше бы, горячей бы

И — чище бы . . .

                 Зубы
Втиснула в губы.
Плакать не буду.

Самую крепость —
В самую мякоть.
Только не плакать.

В братствах бродячих
Мрут, а не плачут,
Жгут, а не плачут.

В пепел и в песню
Мертвого прячут
В братствах бродячих.

— Так первая? Первый ход?
Как в шахматы, значит? Впрочем,
Ведь даже на эшафот
Нас первыми просят . . .

                    — Срочно

Прошу, не глядите! — Взгляд. —
(Вот-вот уже хлынут градом!
Ну как их загнать назад
В глаза?!) — Говорю, не надо

Глядеть!!!

Внятно и громко,
Взгляд в вышину:
— Милый, уйдемте,
Плакать начну!

——————————————

Забыла! Среди копилок
Живых (коммерсантов — тож!)
Белокурый сверкнул затылок:
Маис, кукуруза, рожь!

Все заповеди Синая
Смывая — менады мех! —
Голконда волосяная,
Сокровищница утех —

(Для всех!) Не напрасно копит
Природа, не сплошь скупа!
Из сих белокурых тропик,
Охотники, — где тропа

Назад? Наготою грубой
Дразня и слепя до слез —
Сплошным золотым прелюбом
Смеющимся пролилось.

— Не правда ли? — Льнущий, мнущий
Взгляд. В каждой реснице — зуд.
— И главное — эта гуща!
Жест, скручивающий в жгут.

О, рвущий уже одежды —
Жест! Проще, чем пить и есть —
Усмешка! (Тебе надежда,
Увы, на спасенье есть!)

И — сестрински или братски?
Союзнически: союз!
— Не похоронив — смеяться!
(И похоронив — смеюсь.)

7

И — набережная. Последняя.
Всё. Порознь и без руки,
Чурающимися соседями
Бредем. Со стороны реки —

Плач. Падающую соленую
Ртуть слизываю без забот:
Луны огромной Соломоновой
Слезам не выслал небосвод.

Столб. Отчего бы лбом не стукнуться
В кровь? Вдребезги бы, а не в кровь!
Страшащимися сопреступниками
Бредем. (Убитое — Любовь.)

Брось! Разве это двое любящих?
В ночь? Порознь? С другими спать?
— Вы понимаете, что будущее —
Там? — Запрокидываюсь вспять.

— Спать! — Новобрачными по коврику . . .
— Спать! — Всё не попадаем в шаг,
В такт. Жалобно: — Возьмите под руку!
Не каторжники, чтобы так!..

Ток. (Точно мне душою — на руку
Лег! — На руку рукою.) Ток

Бьет, проводами лихорадочными
Рвет, — на душу рукою лег!

Льнет. Радужное всё! Что радужнее
Слез? Занавесом, чаще бус,
Дождь. — Я таких не знаю набережных
Кончающихся. — Мост, и:

                  — Ну-с?

Здесь? (Дроги поданы.)
Спо — койных глаз
Взлет. — Можно до дому?
В по — следний раз!

8

По — следний мост.
(Руки не отдам, не выну!)
Последний мост,
Последняя мостовина.

Во — да и твердь.
Выкладываю монеты.
День — га за смерть,
Харонова мзда за Лету.

Мо — неты тень
В руке теневой. Без звука
Мо — неты те.
Итак, в теневую руку —

Мо — неты тень.
Без отсвета и без звяка.
Мо — неты — тем.
С умерших довольно маков.

Мост.

Бла — гая часть
Любовников без надежды:
Мост, ты — как страсть:
Условность: сплошное между.

Гнезжусь: тепло,
Ребро — потому и льну так.
Ни до, ни по:
Прозрения промежуток!

Ни рук, ни ног.
Всей костью и всем упором:
Жив только бок,
О смежный теснюсь которым.

Вся жизнь — в боку!
Он — ухо и он же — эхо.
Желтком к белку
Леплюсь, самоедом к меху

Теснюсь, леплюсь,
Мощусь. Близнецы Сиама,
Что — ваш союз?
Та женщина — помнишь: мамой

Звал? — всё и вся
Забыв, в торжестве недвижном
Те — бя нося,
Тебя не держала ближе.

Пойми! Сжились!
Сбылись! На груди баюкал!
Не — брошусь вниз!
Нырять — отпускать бы руку

При — шлось. И жмусь,
И жмусь . . . И неотторжима.
Мост, ты не муж:
Любовник — сплошное мимо!

Мост, ты за нас!
Мы реку телами кормим!
Плю — щом впилась,
Клещом — вырывайте с корнем!

Как плющ! как клещ!
Безбожно! Бесчеловечно!
Бро — сать, как вещь,
Меня, ни единой вещи

Не чтившей в сём
Вещественном мире дутом!
Скажи, что сон!
Что ночь, а за ночью — утро,

Эк — спресс и Рим!
Гренада? Сама не знаю,
Смахнув перин
Монбланы и Гималаи.

Про — гал глубок:
Последнею кровью грею.
Про — слушай бок!
Ведь это куда вернее

Сти — хов . . . Прогрет
Ведь? Завтра к кому наймешься?
Ска — жи, что бред!
Что нет и не будет мосту

Кон — ца . . .
          — Конец.

———————————————

— Здесь? — Детский, божеский
Жест. — Ну-с? — Впилась.
— Е — ще немножечко:
В последний раз!

9

Корпусами фабричными, зычными
И отзывчивыми на зов . . .
Сокровенную, подъязычную
Тайну жен от мужей, и вдов

От друзей — тебе, подноготную
Тайну Евы от древа — вот:
Я не более чем животное,
Кем-то раненное в живот.

Жжет . . . Как будто бы душу сдернули
С кожей! Паром в дыру ушла
Пресловутая ересь вздорная,
Именуемая душа.

Христианская немочь бледная!
Пар! Припарками обложить!
Да ее никогда и не было!
Было тело, хотело жить,

Жить не хочет.

_____

Прости меня! Не хотела!
Вопль вспоротого нутра!
Так смертники ждут расстрела
В четвертом часу утра

За шахматами . . . Усмешкой
Дразня коридорный глаз.
Ведь шахматные же пешки!
И кто-то играет в нас.

Кто? Боги благие? Воры?
Во весь окоем глазка —
Глаз. Красного коридора
Лязг. Вскинутая доска.

Махорочная затяжка.
Сплёв, пожили значит, сплёв.
 . . . По сим тротуарам в шашку
Прямая дорога: в ров

И в кровь. Потайное око:
Луны слуховой глазок . . .
. . . .
И покосившись сбоку:
— Как ты уже далек!

10

Совместный и сплоченный
Вздрог. — Наша молочная!

Наш остров, наш храм,
Где мы по утрам —

Сброд! Пара минутная! —
Справляли заутреню.

Базаром и закисью,
Сквозь-сном и весной . . .
Здесь кофе был пакостный, —
Совсем овсяной!

(Овсом своенравие
Гасить в рысаках!)
Отнюдь не Аравией —
Аркадией пах

Тот кофе . . .

Но как улыбалась нам,
Рядком усадив.
Бывалой и жалостной, —
Любовниц седых

Улыбкою бережной:
Увянешь! Живи!

Безумью, безденежью,
Зевку и любви, —

А главное — юности!
Смешку — без причин,
Усмешке — без умысла,
Лицу — без морщин, —

О, главное — юности!
Страстям не по климату!
Откуда-то дунувшей,
Откуда-то хлынувшей

В молочную тусклую:
— Бурнус и Тунис! —
Надеждам и мускулам
Под ветхостью риз . . .

(Дружочек, не жалуюсь:
Рубец на рубце!)
О, как провожала нас
Хозяйка в чепце

Голландского глаженья . . .

———————————————————

Не довспомнивши, не допонявши,
Точно с праздника уведены . . .

— Наша улица! — Уже не наша . . . —
— Сколько раз по ней . . . — Уже не мы . . . —

— Завтра с западу встанет солнце!
— С Иеговой порвет Давид!
— Что мы делаем? — Расстаемся.
— Ничего мне не говорит

Сверхбессмысленнейшее слово:
Рас — стаемся. — Одна из ста?
Просто слово в четыре слога,
За которыми пустота.

Стой! По-сербски и по-кроатски,
Верно, Чехия в нас чудит?
Рас — ставание. Расставаться . . .
Сверхъестественнейшая дичь!

Звук, от коего уши рвутся,
Тянутся за предел тоски . . .
Расставание — не по-русски!
Не по-женски! Не по-мужски!

Не по-божески! Что мы — овцы,
Раззевавшиеся в обед?
Расставание — по-каковски?
Даже смысла такого нет,

Даже звука! Ну, просто полый
Шум — пилы, например, сквозь сон.

Расставание — просто школы
Хлебникова соловьиный стон,

Лебединый . . .
Но как же вышло?
Точно высохший водоем —
Воздух! Руку о руку слышно.
Расставаться — ведь это гром

На голову . . . Океан в каюту!
Океании крайний мыс!
Эти улицы — слишком круты:
Расставаться — ведь это вниз,

Под гору . . . Двух подошв пудовых
Вздох . . . Ладонь, наконец, и гвоздь!
Опрокидывающий довод:
Расставаться — ведь это врозь,

Мы же — сросшиеся . . .

11

Разом проигрывать —
Чище нет!
Загород, пригород:
Дням конец.

Негам (читай — камням),
Дням, и домам, и нам.

Дачи пустующие! Как мать
Старую — так же чту их.
Это ведь действие — пустовать:
Полое не пустует.

(Дачи, пустующие на треть,
Лучше бы вам сгореть!)

Только не вздрагивать,
Рану вскрыв.
Загород, загород,
Швам разрыв!

Ибо — без лишних слов
Пышных — любовь есть шов.

Шов, а не перевязь, шов — не щит.
— О, не проси защиты! —
Шов, коим мертвый к земле пришит,
Коим к тебе пришита.

(Время покажет еще, каким:
Легким или тройным!)

Так или иначе, друг, — по швам!
Дребезги и осколки!
Только и славы, что треснул сам:
Треснул, а не расползся!

Что под наметкой — живая жиль
Красная, а не гниль!

О, не проигрывает —
Кто рвет!
Загород, пригород:
Лбам развод.

По слободам казнят
Нынче, — мозгам сквозняк!

О, не проигрывает, кто прочь —
В час, как заря займется.
Целую жизнь тебе сшила в ночь
Набело, без наметки.

Так не кори же меня, что вкривь.
Пригород: швам разрыв.

Души неприбранные —
В рубцах!..

Загород, пригород . . .
Яр размах

Пригорода. Сапогом судьбы,
Слышишь — по глине жидкой?
. . . Скорую руку мою суди,
Друг, да живую нитку

Цепкую — как ее ни канай!
По — следний фонарь!

Здесь? Словно заговор —
Взгляд. Низших рас —
Взгляд. — Можно на гору?
В по — следний раз!

12

Частой гривою
Дождь в глаза. — Холмы.
Миновали пригород.
За городом мы.

Есть — да нету нам!
Мачеха — не мать!
Дальше некуда.
Здесь околевать.

Поле. Изгородь.
Брат стоим с сестрой.
Жизнь есть пригород. —
За городом строй!

Эх, проигранное
Дело, господа!
Всё-то — пригороды!
Где же города?!

Рвет и бесится
Дождь. Стоим и рвем.
За три месяца
Первое вдвоем!

И у Иова,
Бог, хотел взаймы?

Да не выгорело:
За городом мы!

————————————————

За городом! Понимаешь? За!
Вне! Перешед вал!
Жизнь — это место, где жить нельзя:
Ев — рейский квартал . . .

Так не достойнее ль во сто крат
Стать Вечным Жидом?
Ибо для каждого, кто не гад,
Ев — рейский погром —

Жизнь. Только выкрестами жива!
Иудами вер!
На прокаженные острова!
В ад! — всюду! — но не в

Жизнь, — только выкрестов терпит, лишь
Овец — палачу!
Право-на-жительственный свой лист
Но — гами топчу!

Втаптываю! За Давидов щит —
Месть! — В месиво тел!
Не упоительно ли, что жид
Жить — не захотел?!

Гетто избранничеств! Вал и ров.
По — щады не жди!
В сём христианнейшем из миров
Поэты — жиды!

13

Так ножи вострят о камень,
Так опилки метлами
Смахивают. Под руками —
Меховое, мокрое.

Где ж вы, двойни:
Сушь мужская, мощь?
Под ладонью —
Слезы, а не дождь!

О каких еще соблазнах —
Речь? Водой — имущество!
После глаз твоих алмазных,
Под ладонью льющихся, —

Нет пропажи
Мне. Конец концу!
Глажу — глажу —
Глажу по лицу.

Такова у нас, Маринок,
Спесь, — у нас, полячек-то.
После глаз твоих орлиных,
Под ладонью плачущих . . .

Плачешь? Друг мой!
Все мое! Прости!

О, как крупно,
Солоно в горсти!

Жестока слеза мужская:
Обухом по темени!
Плачь, с другими наверстаешь
Стыд, со мной потерянный.

Оди — накового
Моря — рыбы! Взмах:
 . . . Мертвой раковиной
Губы на губах.

————————————

В слезах.
Лебеда —
На вкус.
— А завтра,
Когда
Проснусь?

14

Тропою овечьей —
Спуск. Города гам.
Три девки навстречу.
Смеются. Слезам

Смеются, — всем полднем
Недр, гребнем морским!
Смеются!
— недолжным,
Позорным, мужским

Слезам твоим, видным
Сквозь дождь — в два рубца!
Как жемчуг — постыдным
На бронзе бойца.

Слезам твоим первым,
Последним, — о, лей! —
Слезам твоим — перлам
В короне моей!

Глаз явно не туплю.
Сквозь ливень — перюсь.
Венерины куклы,
Вперяйтесь! Союз

Сей более тесен,
Чем влечься и лечь.

Самой Песней Песен
Уступлена речь

Нам, птицам безвестным,
Челом Соломон
Бьет, ибо совместный
Плач — больше, чем сон!

———————————

И в полые волны
Мглы — сгорблен н равн —
Бесследно, безмолвно —
Как тонет корабль.

Прага, 1 февраля — Иловищи, 8 июня 1924

1924

THE TWO OF US

1

There are rhymes in this world:
Uncouple them — and it falls apart.
Homer, you were blind as a bat.
Night — over your craggy head.

Night — your rhapsodic cloak,
Night — over your eyes — a curtain.
Would any sighted person separate
Helen from Achilles?

Helen. Achilles.
Name a more consonant sound.
Yes, against chaos
The world is built

On consonances, that, if uncoupled,
Take revenge (built on consent!)
Upon the infidelity of women
Take revenge — by burning Troy!

Rhapsodist, you were blind as a bat:
Scattered treasure, as if it were junk.
There are rhymes — in *that* world
That were chosen. That will collapse

This one — if you uncouple them. What needs
Holding in rhyme? Helen, growing older!
. . . Achaea's finest man!
The sweetest woman of Sparta!

Alone in the rustle of a myrtle
Forest, in a cithara's dream:
"Helen. Achilles:
A broken pair."

30 June 1924

2

It's not given, that strong with strong
Come to be joined in this world.
Here's how Siegfried and Brunhilda missed each other,
And settled the matter of their marriage with a sword.

United in mutual hatred
— Like buffaloes! — rock face — to rock face.
He rose from the marriage bed, unrecognized,
And unidentified — she slept.

Apart! — even in the marriage bed —
Apart! — even balled into a fist —
Apart! — even in the language of double-entendre —
Late and apart — that's our marriage!

There's an older instance:
The Amazon taken down like a lion —
Here's how they missed each other: the son of Thetis
And a daughter of Ares: Achilles

And Penthesilea.
                    O remember — how from below
She gazed up! an unhorsed rider's
Gaze! not from Olympus, — out the muck
She gazed up — imperious nevertheless!

And, because of that, afterwards, his one
Desire was: to take her to wife out of darkness.

It's not given, that equal — will meet with equal . . .

. . . .

Here's how we — come to miss each other.

3 July 1924

3

In a world, where everyone
Is stunted and in a lather,
I know — one
Equal to me.

In a world, where we
Want for so much,
I know — one
Strong as me.

In a world, where everything —
Is ivy and mold,
I know: one
You — equal in essence

To me.

3 July 1924

ДВОЕ

1

Есть рифмы в мире сём:
Разъединишь — и дрогнет.
Гомер, ты был слепцом.
Ночь — на буграх надбровных.

Ночь — твой рапсодов плащ,
Ночь — на очах — завесой.
Разъединил ли б зрящ
Елену с Ахиллесом?

Елена. Ахиллес.
Звук назови созвучней.
Да, хаосу вразрез
Построен на созвучьях

Мир, и, разъединен,
Мстит (на согласьях строен!)
Неверностями жен
Мстит — и горящей Троей!

Рапсод, ты был слепцом:
Клад рассорил, как рухлядь.
Есть рифмы — в мире том
Подобранные. Рухнет

Сей — разведешь. Что нужд
В рифме? Елена, старься!
. . . Ахеи лучший муж!
Сладостнейшая Спарты!

Лишь шорохом древес
Миртовых, сном кифары:
«Елена: Ахиллес:
Разрозненная пара».

30 июня 1924

2

Не суждено, чтобы сильный с сильным
Соединились бы в мире сем.
Так разминулись Зигфрид с Брунгильдой,
Брачное дело решив мечом.

В братственной ненависти союзной
— Буйволами! — на скалу — скала.
С брачного ложа ушел, неузнан,
И неопознанною — спала.

Порознь! — даже на ложе брачном —
Порознь! — даже сцепясь в кулак —
Порознь! — на языке двузначном —
Поздно и порознь — вот наш брак!

Но и постарше еще обида
Есть: амазонку подмяв как лев —
Так разминулися: сын Фетиды
С дщерью Аресовой: Ахиллес

С Пенфезилеей.
О вспомни — снизу
Взгляд ее! сбитого седока
Взгляд! не с Олимпа уже, — из жижи
Взгляд ее — все ж еще свысока!

Что ж из того, что отсель одна в нем
Ревность: женою урвать у тьмы.

Не суждено, чтобы равный — с равным . . .
. . . .

Так разминовываемся — мы.

3 июля 1924

3

В мире, где всяк
Сгорблен и взмылен,
Знаю — один
Мне равносилен.

В мире, где столь
Многого хощем,
Знаю — один
Мне равномощен.

В мире, где всё —
Плесень и плющ,
Знаю: один
Ты — равносущ

Мне.

3 июля 1924

AN ISLAND

There's an island. Wrested from the Nereids
By an underground heave.
Virgin ground. Which no one
Has yet mapped or opened up.

Fringed with ferns and hidden
In sea-foam. — The way? Some passage?
I just know: it's still unclaimed
Anywhere, except in your

Columbian eyes. Two palms:
Clarity! — That vanishes. — At the stroke
Of a condor . . .
                              (In the sleeping-car
— That's enough — about islands!)

An hour's, maybe — a week's
Sailing (if I can manage it — a year!)
I just know: it's still unclaimed
Anywhere, except in the latitudes

Of the future . . .

5 July 1924

UNDER A SHAWL

Sealed, like the mouth of an oracle —
Your mouth, augers for many.
Woman, what have you concealed from the guards
Between your tongue and the roof of your mouth?

Looking into the ages, not with your eyes
But with their sockets, like brimming cauldrons!
Woman, what sort of pit have you dug
And roofed over with turf?

No idol with even a hundred heathen
Temples — could be more imperious.
Woman, what have you pulled out of the fire
Of languor and one-night stands?

Woman, you spread yourself in secret, like a shawl,
In a shawl, like a secret, you linger.
Set apart — like a single surviving
Spruce on a misted summit.

It seems I question you as a dead
Soul, who has sipped at the root . . .
Woman, what do you have beneath your shawl?
— The future!

8 November 1924

ПОД ШАЛЬЮ

Запечатленный, как рот оракула —
Рот твой, гадавший многим.
Женщина, что от дозору спрятала
Меж языком и нёбом?

Уж не глазами, а в вечность дырами
Очи, котлом ведёрным!
Женщина, яму какую вырыла
И заложила дёрном?

Располагающий ста кумирнями
Идол — не столь заносчив.
Женщина, что у пожара вырвала
Нег и страстей двунощных?

Женщина, в тайнах, как в шалях, ширишься,
В шалях, как в тайнах, длишься.
Отъединенная — как счастливица-
Ель на вершине мглистой.

Точно усопшую вопрошаю,
Душу, к корням пригубившую . . .
Женщина, что у тебя под шалью?
— Будущее!

8 ноября 1924

* * *

All by herself — Helen gazes over the rooftops
Of Troy! In her stunned pupils
Four provinces lie drained of blood
And hope for a hundred centuries.

All by herself — Helen acknowledges
The nuptial slaughter: her nakedness
Stripped four Arabys of all sultriness
And five oceans of their pearls.

All by herself, Helen — waits to unclasp
Her hands! — but marvels at the swarm
Of heirs to the throne left homeless
And their forefathers, rushing into battle.

All by herself, Helen — can't depend on the appeal
Of her lips! — but marvels at the ditch
Piled with heirs to the throne:
At the end of a hundred familial lines.

But no, it's not Helen! Not that twice-taken
Predator, that pestilential drought.
What a treasure house lies squandered
By you, who look us in the eye — the way

Not even Helen at this splendid banquet
Dare look her slaves in the eye:
Much less the gods. — "A land left unmanned
By a foreign woman! Still grovels — at her feet!"

11 November 1924

* * *

I sang like arrows and eels,
Racing underfoot
With the sound of riven satin.
— I sang! — and a wholly padded wall
Could not restrain me
Nor could the world.
Because I tore one
Gift from the gods: flight!

I sang like arrows.
The body?
Was not my concern!

8 November 1924

AN ATTEMPT AT JEALOUSY

How is your life with another, —
Simpler, is it? — One stroke of an oar!—
And as easily as some coastline
Your memory of me

Recedes, like a floating island
(In the sky — not the water!)
Souls, souls! should be your sisters,
Not your mistress—es!

How is your life with a *simple*
Woman? *Without* your goddess?
Your Majesty dethroned, over-
Thrown (by a single slip-up),

How is your life — keeping busy —
Holed up? How do you even — get up?
With the customs of undying banality
How do you manage, poor man?

"Enough of these eruptions —
And scenes! I'll get my own house."
How is life with just anyone —
My chosen one!

With more appropriate, more edible —
Food? Fed up — not your fault . . .
How is your life with a molehill —
You, who trampled Sinai!

How is your life with a foreigner,
A local? Close to your rib — a dear?
Doesn't shame lash your head
Like the reins of Zeus?

How is your life — are you well —
Able? Do you sing ever — how?
With the curse of undying conscience
How do you manage, poor man?

How is your life with a commodity
Of the market? Finding her rent — steep?
After the marble of Carrara
How is life with the dust

Of plaster? (A God—hewn from
Blocks — and now utterly shattered!)
How is your life with the hundredth-thousandth —
You, who knew Lilith!

Does your novelty of the market
Satisfy? Grown cool to enchantment,
How is your life with an earthly
Woman, with no sixth

Sense?
        Well, I declare: are you happy?
No? In a shallow draining whirl —
How is your life, darling? Is it harder,
As it is for me, with another?

19 November 1924

ПОПЫТКА РЕВНОСТИ

Как живется вам с другою, —
Проще ведь? — Удар весла! —
Линией береговою
Скоро ль память отошла

Обо мне, плавучем острове
(По небу — не по водам)!
Души, души! — быть вам сестрами,
Не любовницами — вам!

Как живется вам с простою
Женщиною? Без божеств?
Государыню с престола
Свергши (с оного сошед),

Как живется вам — хлопочется —
Ежится? Встается — как?
С пошлиной бессмертной пошлости
Как справляетесь, бедняк?

«Судорог да перебоев —
Хватит! Дом себе найму».
Как живется вам с любою —
Избранному моему!

Свойственнее и сьедобнее —
Снедь? Приестся — не пеняй . . .

Как живется вам с подобием —
Вам, поправшему Синай!

Как живется вам с чужою,
Здешнею? Ребром — люба?
Стыд Зевесовой вожжою
Не охлестывает лба?

Как живется вам — здоровится —
Можется? Поется — как?
С язвою бессмертной совести
Как справляетесь, бедняк?

Как живется вам с товаром
Рыночным? Оброк — крутой?
После мраморов Каррары
Как живется вам с трухой

Гипсовой? (Из глыбы высечен
Бог — и начисто разбит!)
Как живется вам с сто-тысячной —
Вам, познавшему Лилит!

Рыночною новизною
Сыты ли? К волшбам остыв,
Как живется вам с земною
Женщиною, без шестых

Чувств?..

Ну, за голову: счастливы?
Нет? В провале без глубин —
Как живется, милый? Тяжче ли,
Так же ли, как мне с другим?

19 ноября 1924

* * *

A blizzard sweeps the floors.
All explosion and rift! —

And on my colorful cheerful scarf —
Tears of sharp salt,
Pearls coarsely ground.

19 November 1924

* * *

Вьюга наметает в полы.
Всё разрывы да расколы! —

И на шарф цветной веселый —
Слезы острого рассола,
Жемчуг крупного размола.

19 ноября 1924

A DREAM

1

I buried myself, dropped off — and then, watched as if from
A thousand-foot staircase with no railing.
With the rapacity of an investigator or detective
A dream dug up — all my secrets.

Volcanoes — that seemed firmly to have died down —
Don't trust such passions to die!
Alertly — like an inspector of the heart's
Chambers — it seems Morpheus paces.

You! the collectively undistinguished!
There's no call to launch yourselves off roofs!
If only you knew how easily you can become
Sultry by merely reclining in a feather-bed!

You collapse! Like a crushed shell —
Life with its load of husbands and wives.
Alert as an aviator over slumbering but hostile
Territory — over my soul a dream flies.

My body, with all its doors locked —
In vain! — shots still ring through me.
With the precision of a barber or surgeon
A dream has probed — all my wounds!

And laid me open! from the gallery, under a cupola,
No way to escape the notice of my own
Prophetic eyes. Like a compromised confessor
A dream has told — all my secrets!

24 November 1924

2

In my brain a pothole has opened up, —
Three centuries until the spring!
I go to bed, as I would to a theatre-box:
Just to see these dreams:

To see: David's paradise
And to hold the helmet of Achilles
Sacred, — to see no more of walls!
I go to bed — for this.

Apart from Martin
Zedeka — I'm not likely to find anyone!
I don't care for comforters:
Any more than for drifting snow!

Pampering you, — with feminine adulations'
Fluff, the clasp of arms and legs.
Like a woman who smothers her infant
Of three days' in her sleep.

To sleep! The ceiling taken down
Like a box! Washed down with blue!
I go to bed as if into a hole in ice:
To drown you, — not myself!

The transoceanic tropic
Rot, the silt — of Hindustan . . .
I go to bed, as I would to a precipice:
To my comforter — *with no* railing!

26 November 1924

СОН

1

Врылась, забылась — и вот как с тысяче-
футовой лестницы без перил.
С хищностью следователя и сыщика
Все мои тайны — сон перерыл.

Сопки — казалось бы прочно замерли —
Не доверяйте смертям страстей!
Зорко — как следователь по камере
Сердца — расхаживает Морфей.

Вы! собирательное убожество!
Не обрывающиеся с крыш!
Знали бы, как на перинах лёжачи
Преображаешься и паришь!

Рухаешь! Как скорлупою треснувшей —
Жизнь с ее грузом мужей и жен.
Зорко как летчик над вражьей местностью
Спящею — над душою сон.

Тело, что все свои двери заперло —
Тщетно! — уж ядра поют вдоль жил.
С точностью сбирра и оператора
Все мои раны — сон перерыл!

Вскрыта! ни щелки в райке, под куполом,
Где бы укрыться от вещих глаз
Собственных. Духовником подкупленным
Все мои тайны — сон перетряс!

24 ноября 1924

2

В мозгу ухаб пролёжан, —
Три века до весны!
В постель иду, как в ложу:
Затем, чтоб видеть сны:

Сновидеть: рай Давидов
Зреть и Ахиллов шлем
Священный, — стен не видеть!
В постель иду — затем.

Разведены с Мартыном
Задекою — не все!
Не доверяй перинам:
С сугробами в родстве!

Занежат, — лести женской
Пух, рук и ног захват.
Как женщина младенца
Трехдневного заспят.

Спать! Потолок как короб
Снять! Синевой запить!
В постель иду как в прорубь:
Вас, — не себя топить!

Заокеанских тропик
Прель, Индостана — ил . . .
В постель иду как в пропасть:
Перины — без перил!

26 ноября 1924

THE SIGNS

As if I'd dragged a mountain in my skirts —
My whole body aches!
I know it must be love by the ache
Down the length of my body.

As if the ground ahead had cleared
Itself of any storm.
I know it must be love by the distance
Of everyone and everything that's near.

As if a shaft had burrowed into me
To the bottom, to its tar.
I know it must be love by my muscles'
Moaning down the length of my

Body. Caught in a draft
As if in the mane of a Hun:
I know it must be love by the derangement
Of my truest-tuned strings,

My most guttural, — most guttural ravines'
Rust, living salt.
I know it must be love by my glottis,
No! — by the vibrato
Down the length of my body!

29 November 1924

ПРИМЕТЫ

Точно гору несла в подоле —
Всего тела боль!
Я любовь узнаю по боли
Всего тела вдоль.

Точно поле во мне разъяли
Для любой грозы.
Я любовь узнаю по дали
Всех и вся вблизи.

Точно нору во мне прорыли
До основ, где смоль.
Я любовь узнаю по жиле,
Всего тела вдоль

Стонущей. Сквозняком как гривой
Овеваясь, гунн:
Я любовь узнаю по срыву
Самых верных струн

Горловых, — горловых ущелий
Ржавь, живая соль.
Я любовь узнаю по щели,
Нет! — по трели
Всего тела вдоль!

29 ноября 1924

* * *

A yagatan? A firing squad?
Something more modest, — why be so loud!

Pain, familiar, as my palm — to my eyes,
As the name of my own child —
Is to my mouth.

1 December 1924

* * *

Ятаган? Огонь?
Поскромнее, — куда как громко!

Боль, знакомая, как глазам — ладонь,
Как губам —
Имя собственного ребенка.

1 декабря 1924

* * *

I live — without touching.
I can't move mountains.
Ask the amputee,
Who says: This is what it is to live.

It's not ours — it's God's
Mountain — Jehovah's!
Caldera and lair, —
We can live without many things.

1 December 1924

THE FLOOR POLISHERS' SONG

Thrashers-threshers,
Floor polishers-pesterers,
Red calico figures,
Fringed trousers.

Taking Stephan or Osip —
No mark, no print.
— Whoever the devil brings us,
We're floor polishers, always.

Faultlessly, persistently,
We apply ourselves to the floor.
Over the parquet, with an "ah",
We send dead moths on their way.

Red-feathered sandpipers,
Dancing floor polishers!

Rumbling-pounders,
For us any room is too close.
Grandmother's ring's missing — we
Floor polishers made off with it.

We turn up the heat,
We make it glow.
. . . We touch!
. . . We pilfer!

We floor polishers give nothing up:
Twisted first one way and another!
We roll right up and propose:
"Please, come to tea with us!"

That's not floor polish on your
Ash floors we're spreading.
That's sweat and blood on your
Ash floors we're using as wax:

To wax them white!
Make the furniture creak!

Speak softly, softer than chamois . . .
With floor polishers in the house —
Weep! It looks like, while dancing,
We broke the nose off your goddess.

That goddess — the marble one,
Dress her up — a la Lamonoff,
No one will be the wiser she's marble —
We beat everyone about the head and shoulders!

Naked, barefoot.
Until we blister!

Floor polishing is an unhealthy business:
Dancing ourselves into a fever!
From which our faces are grown pale,
All our blood pooled in our feet.

Using a foot we write,
Using a foot we plow.
Whoever's taller would be —
Who we choose to dance with.

O with five gnarled toes —
Like the foot of a Lord!
From the foyer — down the narrow hall —
And you're done for!

Unconcerned, break free
Of the stitch in your chest!
. . . Hope for a six-
Toed floor polisher.

Holding a ball is nothing new for us!
Are the doors — all locked?
It's red calico because — blood
Doesn't show on red calico!

Ours or yours —
Lie down and don't ask.

It's the master's business to track
Mud, with no thought for our wax —
The floor polishers' business — to erase
His tracks with elbow-grease.

And that grease is so fine!
— Rosin, new snow, is falling! —

Floor-healers — floor-flyers,
Floor polishers — flashers-by,
Flying-trousers,
Noble heel-clickers,

We're not shaking the bugs out
Of the meat-dealer's little pillow,
Along the parquetry we're rousting out —
Ferreting out the masters!

A terrific business,
Red-hot,
Red Guard!

———————

Hurry up, on your toes, sergeants!
The floor polishers have knifed a merchant.

Come see what you've never dreamed of:
The floor polishers have done in a merchant!

18 December 1924

ПОЛОТЁРСКАЯ

Колотёры-молотёры,
Полотёры-полодёры,
Кумашный стан,
Бахромчатый штан.

Что Степан у вас, что Осип —
Ни приметы, ни следа.
— Нас нелегкая приносит,
Полотеров, завсегда.

Без вины навязчивые,
Мы полы наващиваем.
По паркетам вз'ахивая,
Мы молей вымахиваем.

Кулик краснопер,
Пляши, полотер!

Колотилы-громыхалы,
Нам все комнаты тесны.
Кольцо бабкино пропало —
Полотеры унесли.

Нажариваем.
Накаливаем.
. . . Пошариваем!
. . . Пошаливаем!

С полотеров взятки гладки:
Катай вдоль да поперек!
Как подкатимся вприсядку:
«Пожалуйте на чаёк!»

Не мастикой ясеневы
Вам полы намасливаем.
Потом-кровью ясеневы
Вам полы наласниваем:

Вощи до-бела!
Трещи, мебеля!

Тише сажи, мягче замши . . .
Полотеров взявши в дом —
Плачь! Того гляди, плясамши,
Нос богине отобьем.

Та богиня — мраморная,
Нарядить — от Ламановой,
Не гляди, что мраморная —
Всем бока наламываем!

Гол, бос.
Чтоб жглось!

Полотерско дело вредно:
Пляши, в пот себя вогнав!
Оттого и ликом бледны,
Что вся кровь у нас в ногах.

Ногой пишем,
Ногой пашем.
Кто повыше —
Тому пляшем.

О пяти корявых пальцах —
Как и барская нога!
Из прихожей — через зальце —
Вот и вся вам недолга!

Знай, откалывай
До кола в груди!
. . . Шестипалого
Полотера жди.

Нам балы давать не внове!
Двери — все ли на ключе?
А кумач затем — что крови
Не видать на кумаче!

Нашей ли, вашей ли —
Ляжь да не спрашивай.

Как господско дело грязью
Следить, лоску не жалеть —
Полотерско дело — мазью
Те следочки затереть.

А уж мазь хороша!
— Занялась пороша! —

Полодёры-полодралы,
Полотёры-пролеталы,
Разлет-штаны,
Паны-шаркуны,

Из перинки прасоловой
Не клопов вытрясываем,
По паркетам взгаркивая —
Мы господ вышаркиваем!

Страсть-дела,
Жар-дела,
Красная гвардия!

———————

Поспешайте, сержанты резвые!
Полотеры купца зарезали.

Получайте, чего не грезили:
Полотеры купца заездили.

18 декабря 1924

* * *

Larger than an organ, more raucous than a tambourine
A sigh — the same for everyone:
Oh, when it's hard, and ah, when it's lovely,
And when it doesn't come easy—eh!

Ah with the Empyrean and oh over the plough,
And, admit it, poet,
The Muse has no more
Than these: ahs and ohs.

The richest, truest rhyme,
The most liquid tone.
This was Solomon — before
A blushing Shulamite — ah.

Ah: broken heart,
Syllable, we breathe as we die.
Ah, the curtain — suddenly — opening,
Oh: this horse-collar.

Word-finder, smooth-talker,
Running spigot of words,
Eh, if you've heard once — how
The Polovetsian camp ah-ed in the night!

And he crouched, like a beast hunched up . . .
In moss, in sounds of fur:

Ah — yes, isn't it a gypsy encampment
— A village! — with a moon overhead!

A stallion, gnashing the full measure of his teeth,
Snorting, anticipating the race.
Oleg who ran up on his horse's skull,
Who commanded a song —

Of Pushkin. And — with arrows burning and flying —
Into a dark mass of ancient warriors —
Those invincible cries of the flesh:
Oh! — Eh! — Ah!

23 December 1924

TO LIFE

1

You won't lay a hand on my high color —
Which is strong — as any flooding river!
You hunt, but I won't yield,
You, a pursuer, I, pure flight.

You won't lay a hand on my soul while it lives!
Pursued at a gallop, at full-tilt —
Nipping — its own tendon
And severing it, my steed is an

Arabian.

25 December 1924

2

You won't lay a hand on my soul while it lives,
I won't yield like goose down.
Life, that so often rhymes with: lie, —
As my singer's ear is infallible!

Inconceivable to any older inhabitant!
Let me go, pass to other shores!
Life, that so clearly rhymes with fat:
Life: stop it! life: don't press me.

It's cruel to shackle my legs
In irons, so rust works itself to the bone!
Life: a knife-edge on which your beloved
Dances.
         — Weary of waiting for the knife!

28 December 1924

1925

THE CONSECRATION

He failed to warm the water through and through
In its fount, it was freezing — as need be —
That little-father, who consecrated me.
In the shallow wedding-ladle

He failed to sweeten the wine through and through —
The spirit mustn't trifle with coupling!
That little-father, who consecrated me
To the difficult business of marriage:

That little-father, who officiated.
(Revived, the ballerina learned,
Your sap is poison, Upas-tree,
Offered in a shallow wedding-ladle

And tasted . . .)
             — To endless ardor,
To the sticky niche of a poet I was
Consecrated — you consecrated me
With water that was un-warmed, straight

Out of the river, — to greater things, than
Usually fall to women's charge —
Consecrated — you consecrated me
With this un-sweetened calamity:

With this unadulterated wine.
When I choke — remind me!

What fire should I singe myself with?
When all my passions seem like water

At room temperature. Right three times over
That little-father, who pruned me back.
What poisons should I learn to fear?
When all venom — seems like water

Boiled and sterile. To me, what is fate
With its patrimonial terrors —
When, naturally, running down my cheeks,
These tears — seem a sweet water!

But you, who consecrated me
With the water of an ecstatic Saul
(Like Saul, raising his crutch,
To command the faithless to attention) —

Pray, that you be forgiven —
By God.

1 January 1925

* * *

Alive, it's not dead,
This demon in me!
In my body as in a cargo-hold,
In myself as in a prison.

All the world's — walls.
Exit is — an axe.
("All the world's — a stage,"
An actor prattles).

And he wasn't cunning,
That lame fool.
In the body — as in a rumor,
In the body — as in a toga!

May you live many years!
Alive — value it!
(As only poets do
To the bone — by some lie!)

No, it's not for us to step out,
My singing brethren,
In the body as in the quilted
Smocks of our fathers.

Better is what we deserve.
We wither in this warmth.

In the body — as in a close room,
In ourselves — as in a caldera.

We can't keep the transitory
Splendors.
In the body — as in a swamp,
In the body — as in a vault,

In the body — as in farthest
Exile. — Withered away!
In the body — as in the dark,
In my temples — as in the vise

Of an iron mask.

5 January 1925

* * *

Squeezed into this basin of my
Existence, in this stupor of slackness,
Buried alive under this avalanche
Of days — as if in penal servitude, I let go of life.

These are my winter-quarters, deathly and sealed.
Death: a hoarfrost on my beautiful lips —
I have no wish for better health
From God or come the spring.

11 January 1925

* * *

Существования котловиною
Сдавленная, в столбняке глушизн,
Погребенная заживо под лавиною
Дней — как каторгу избываю жизнь.

Гробовое, глухое мое зимовье.
Смерти: инея на уста-красны —
Никакого иного себе здоровья
Не желаю от Бога и от весны.

11 января 1925

* * *

What, my Muse? Is she still alive?
Like one captive taps her comrade
On the ear, the little pit, gouged by a finger
— What my Muse? Will she be here long?

Neighbors, entangled by their hearts.
Prisoners tapping out their exchanges.

What my Muse? Is she still alive?
Impossible to tell from the eyes of desire,
What's true or covered by a smile,
Or by the neighbors, one rack to the right

— What, dear boy? Did we manage a brief hour?
A wink passed through the sick ward.

Eh, my affairs! Eh, transparent, if somewhat gauzy!
Like those aerial battles above the Armies,
All scribbled over with summer-lightning slants,
Eyebrows passing flashes.

In a funnel of dissipated haze —
Soldiers passing trash-talk.

Come, my Muse! A rhyme at least!
Of cheek — like Ilium flaring up —

To cheek: "No regrets! Loosening
All my connections — Death! Later, then?"

My sweet last bed's —
Last exchange of embraces.

15 January 1925

ЧТО, МУЗА МОЯ! ЖИВА ЛИ ЕЩЕ?..

Что, Муза моя! Жива ли еще?
Так узник стучит к товарищу
В слух, в ямку, перстом продолбленную
— Что Муза моя? Надолго ли ей?

Соседки, сердцами спутанные.
Тюремное перестукиванье.

Что Муза моя? Жива ли еще?
Глазами не знать желающими,
Усмешкою правду кроющими,
Соседскими, справа-коечными

— Что, братец? Часочек выиграли?
Больничное перемигиванье.

Эх, дело мое! Эх, марлевое!
Так небо боев над Армиями,
Зарницами вкось исчёрканное,
Ресничное пересвёркиванье.

В воронке дымка рассеянного —
Солдатское пересмеиванье.

Ну, Муза моя! Хоть рифму еще!
Щекой — Илионом вспыхнувшею

К щеке: «Не крушись! Расковывает
Смерть — узы мои! До скорого ведь?»

Предсмертного ложа свадебного —
Последнее перетрагиванье.

15 января 1925

* * *

Into grey — my temples,
Into a ditch — my soldier,
— Sky! — like the sea I bleed into you.
So with every syllable —
At your secret glance
I turn,
I primp.

Into a skirmish — my Scythian,
Into flagellation — my Kh'yst,
— Sea! — like the sky I enter you.
So with every line —
At your secret signal
I halt,
I listen up.

At every line: stop!
At every turn — treasure.
— Eye! — like light I settle into you,
I melt. As longing
On a guitar fret
I retune myself,
I restring myself.

Marriage lies — not in down
But in the quills — of swans!
Marriages that are divisive, and diverse!

So at the mark of my dash —
As at a secret sign
Your eyebrows rise —
Can you trust me?

Not in this weak tea
Of rumor — with my breath so strong.
And my stock — so considerable!
Under your thumb
Like the Lord's wafer
I am ground,
Broken in two.

22 January 1925

* * *

Having haggled for a stirrup —
Remember your raven mount!
I am as beyond retrieving as time,
But retrievable as you, seasons

Of the year, sharing the business
Of my family with the first person I meet,
Indifferent as eternity,
But passionate as the first days

Of spring . . . intoxicated on my own
Song like the night — on the nightingale,
Irretrievable as any dying
Breed (of which the poet

Heine sang, — in my secret marriage:
Sweeter than a visitor and closer than a brother . . .)
Irretrievable as the Rhine's own
Dreaming and deadly treasure.

Pure-gold — unalloyed,
Pure-silver — Wagner? — chase me!
I am irretrievable as the glory
Of our Russian . . .

19 February 1925

* * *

Променявши на стремя —
Поминайте коня ворона!
Невозвратна как время,
Но возвратна как вы, времена

Года, с первым из встречных
Предающая дело родни,
Равнодушна как вечность,
Но пристрастна как первые дни

Весен . . . собственным пеньем
Опьяняясь как ночь — соловьем,
Невозвратна как племя
Вымирающее (о нем

Гейне пел, — брак мой тайный:
Слаще гостя и ближе, чем брат . . .)
Невозвратна как Рейна
Сновиденный убийственный клад.

Чиста-злата — нержавый,
Чиста-серебра — Вагнер? — нырни!
Невозвратна как слава
Наша русская . . .

19 февраля 1925

* * *

Dis—tance: versts, miles . . .
We are set — apart, seated — apart,
So we will behave quietly
At our two ends of the earth.

Dis—tance: versts, prospects . . .
We are peeled apart, unsoldered,
Our two hands spread, crucified,
By those who don't know — we are

A fusion of inspiration and tendons . . .
Who can't set us at odds — who dropped us,
Buried us . . .
                Wall and ditch.
Who re-settled us as eagles — co—

Conspirators: versts, prospects . . .
Who failed to thwart us — who lost us, bit by bit.
Who shunted us off as orphans
Into the wastes of earth's expanse.

Already, what is it — March?!
Who cut us — like a deck of cards!

24 March 1925

* * *

Рас — стояние: версты, мили . . .
Нас рас — ставили, рас — садили,
Чтобы тихо себя вели
По двум разным концам земли.

Рас — стояние: версты, дали . . .
Нас расклеили, распаяли,
В две руки развели, распяв,
И не знали, что это — сплав

Вдохновений и сухожилий . . .
Не рассорили — рассорили,
Расслоили . . .
                    Стена да ров.
Расселили нас, как орлов-

Заговорщиков: версты, дали . . .
Не расстроили — растеряли.
По трущобам земных широт
Рассовали нас, как сирот.

Который уж, ну который — март?!
Разбили нас — как колоду карт!

24 марта 1925

* * *

I bow, with my regards, to the Russian rye,
To the field, where an old woman shields her eyes.
My friend! Rains fall beyond my window,
Troubles and blessings into my heart . . .

You, in your own melody of rains and troubles
Are another Homer — caught up in your hexameters,
Lend me a hand — for all the world, for writing!
Here — both mine are full, are never idle.

Prague, 7 May 1925

* * *

Русской ржи от меня поклон,
Полю, где баба застится . . .
Друг! Дожди за моим окном,
Беды и блажи на сердце . . .

Ты в погудке дождей и бед —
То ж, что Гомер в гекзаметре.
Дай мне руку — на весь тот свет!
Здесь мои — обе заняты.

7 мая 1925

1927

NEW YEAR'S

An Elegy for Rilke

Happy New Year
        — New World — New Land — New Home!
           — New Light — New Border — New Eve!
My first letter to your New
— My misunderstanding, to think it might be "green" —
(Lush — pastoral) your resonant, sonorous place
Like Aeolus' empty tower.
My first letter to you from the past,
Where, without you, I languish,
From Mother Earth, that for you now is simply one
Of the stars . . . Our conventions at leave-taking, of distancing,
By which a beloved becomes a someone,
An unbelievable person, merely fabulous.
Shall I tell you how I learned of your?
No earthquake, no avalanche,
A man walked in — someone — (you —
Are who I adored). — A sad story.
— In the News and the Daily. — Would you write something?
— Where? — In the mountains. (A window onto fir branches,
A sheet.) — You haven't seen the newspapers?
Will you write us something? — No. — But . . . — Please, spare me.
Aloud: It would be hard. Inwardly: I won't give him up.
— In a sanatorium. (In a rented heaven).
— When? — Yesterday, day before yesterday, I don't remember.

Coming to the Alcazar? — No, I won't be.
Aloud: My family. Inwardly: Anything but — some Judas.

Happy New Year! (Starting tomorrow!) —
Shall I tell you what I did on learning of . . . ?
Shh . . . a slip of my tongue. Out of habit.
When I was always the one to put life and death in italics,
As if they were the most idle gossip.
I didn't do anything, but something
Happened, without leaving so much as an echo
Or shadow!
        So — how did you go?
Your heart — how did it break and not fly
Apart? As if drawn by Oryol trotters,
As if by eagles, *you said*, flying, no less,
Was it that breathtaking — or more?
Sweeter? With no more of life's highs, or lows,
For those — who've flown behind real Russian eagles.
Though we were blood-coupled to this world:
Whoever has been to Russia — has seen the next world
In this. It makes for a smooth transition!
If I utter the words life and death with a latent
Smirk — you widen yours to meet it!
If I utter the words life and death with footnotes,
With asterisks (hoping there might be some night yet:
Instead of this cerebral hemisphere —
Starlit!)
        Friend, don't let me forget to say:
If some letters now
Come in Russian, and not German —

It's not because, as they say nowadays, everything's
Run to ruin, or that the dead are (expected) to swallow anything —
Without complaint — but to say that our *next* world,
— at thirteen, at Novodevichy, I
Knew: is not dumbstruck, but speaks in every tongue.

If I ask, sadly: will you
Never want to know again, what's Russian for
Nest? What's the single, fully-
Closed rhyme upon: star?

Do I wander? But nothing
Can be found — to distract me from you.
Every thought, each, Du Lieber,
Syllable leads to you — whatever
Its meaning (whether German's more nearly my native tongue than Russian,
Let my first true words be uttered with the tongues of Angels!) — and there's
No place you've not been, no, save one: the grave.
It all seems as if it never was, and all is as it was,
— Really, about me, nothing at all? —
Where are you, Rainer, and how are you?
Tell me, without fail, I insist —
Everything about your first glimpse of our universe
(That is, of a poet left behind
In it) and the last — of our planet,
Only once is it given you to see — as a whole!
Some encounter, not of a poet with his dust, or a soul with its body
(To distinguish such parts is to insult them both)
But your encounter, of you in yourself, of you with yourself even,
— To be taken by Zeus doesn't mean he's done you an honor —

Of Castor — of you in yourself — with Pollux.
Of marble — of you with yourself, with a slender grass blade,
No parting and no meeting — a mere confrontation
Of witnesses: as nearly a parting as a first
Meeting.
        How did you fix your gaze
On your own hand (at the trace — on it — of ink)
From your several (how many?) million miles —
Infinite, pre-temporal
Altitude above the crystal-levels
Of the Mediterranean — and other saucers.
It all seems like it never was, and all is as it will be
As it is for me in these outskirts.
It all seems like it never was, and all is as it is already
— What do you, conscripted, you-called-away care how this final week
Of the year runs out! — and where *else* is one to gaze,
Elbows on the balcony rail,
From this — if not to the next world, and from that next
If not back to the much-suffering this.
In Bellevue, I live. A small village of nests
And branches. Enough to catch the eye of a realtor:
Bellevue. A cell with a beautiful view
Of Paris — a palace of Gallic chimera —
Of Paris — and a bit beyond . . .
Resting your elbows on the scarlet rail
How absurd to you (some would say, may) "must seem,"
(I would say, surely) *must be*, from your matchless altitude,
Our Bellevues and Belvederes!

I wander. In detail. In haste.
New Year's is upon us. To what, with whom, shall I offer toasts

Across a table? With what? With cotton wadding —
For foam. To what? Let the clock strike — and why am I even here?
What am I to do in the New Year's racket
With this internal rhyme: Rainer — no more?
If you, such an eye, go dark,
Life's not life, death not death,
Meaning — darkens as I may come to know in time, should we ever come
                                                                    face to face! —
Not in life, not in death, — but in some third realm, some new
Aspect. So, to that, then, (having strewn out all the straw of custom —
As the twenty-sixth year of our century passes
Into the twenty-seventh — my privilege
To see it out with you, to see it in with you!)
Over some table, too wide to see across,
Shall I salute you with a quiet clink,
Glass to glass? No — not just our tavern-ware:
Me against *you*, two givens moving into rhyme:
A third realm.
                    Across a table where a cross marks your place.
How many places — in the country, so much space
Out of town! for whom else, if not for us,
Does a bush — incline? Places — that are ours,
And nobody else's! All the leaves! All the needles!
Places of your encounters with me (of your encounters with yourself).
(I'm prepared to attend even some awful mass-rally with you —
Should I admit that?) not to mention the other places! or the months!
Or the weeks! Or the rainy, unpeopled
Suburbs! Or the mornings! Or altogether everything else
Not yet broken into by nightingales!

Likely, I see badly, from my pit,
Likely, you see better, higher up:
Nothing ever worked out between us.
So little, so clearly and simply
Nothing, nothing to suit our capacity or stature
— Useless even to count the loss.
Nothing, except — expect nothing
Out of the ordinary, (how clumsy of you to be out
Of ordinary time!) — but in what time would you arrive
If you could?
        It's an old refrain:
Even nothing plus something is
Something — even if only from a distance — a shadow
Of a shadow! Nothing: that hour, that day,
That house — even a prisoner condemned in his manacles,
Has the memory of: those lips!
Or do such things count for too much?
Out of all *that,* a single *world*
Was ours, as we ourselves were just a reflection
Of ourselves, — for all this — all *that* light!

From my barren suburb — I wish you
Happy new place, Rainer, world, Rainer!
To the furthermost point of proof —
Happy new eye, Rainer, ear, Rainer!

Anything would have been an obstacle
To you: a passion, a friendship.
Happy new sound, dear Echo!
Happy new echoes, dear Sound!

How many times seated on a school bench:
What are the mountains there? What are the rivers?
Are they lovely, those landscapes without visitors?
I wasn't wrong, was I, Rainer — Heaven — is mountainous,
Stormy? Free of all claims, all dower —
There's not a single heaven, but beyond it lies another
Heaven? In terraces? As I judge by the Tatras —
Heaven cannot fail to be
An amphitheater. (A curtain lowered on someone . . .)
I wasn't mistaken, Rainer, God is — *a spreading*
Baobab? No Sun King —
And not just one God? But beyond him another
God?

      How are you writing, in your new place?
But if you *are* — your poems *are:* for you yourself are —
Poetry! How is your writing, in that good life,
With no table for your elbow, no brow for your hand,
(Your cupped hand).

                 — Send me some news of yourself, in your
                   usual, undecipherable scrawl!
Rainer, how do you find the new rhymes?
But, to decline the word
Rhyme — properly — what's Death — if not a whole new
Series of Rhyme?

           It's nowhere to go: a language mastered.
A whole new series of meanings and
Assonance.

       — Goodbye! Until we meet!
I don't know — that we will, but — let's agree to.
Beyond the earth that lies before me —

Beyond the seas, Rainer, beyond the last of me!

So we don't lose touch — drop me a note ahead of time.
Happy new tracings of sound, Rainer!

Up the ladders of the sky, climb with your bread and wine . . .
Happy new gesture, Rainer!

— So nothing spills on it, I lift mine — level, on my palm. —
Above the Rhone and Rarogne, above the manifest
And total separation, this I have addressed:
Rainer — Maria — Rilke — for delivery, into his hands.

Bellevue
February 7, 1927.

НОВОГОДНЕЕ

С Новым годом — светом — краем — кровом!
Первое письмо тебе на новом
— Недоразумение, что злачном —
(Злачном — жвачном) месте зычном, месте звучном
Как Эолова пустая башня.
Первое письмо тебе с вчерашней,
На которой без тебя изноюсь,
Родины, теперь уже с одной из
Звезд . . . Закон отхода и отбоя,
По которому любимая любою
И небывшею из небывалой.
Рассказать, как про твою узнала?
Не землетрясенье, не лавина.
Человек вошел — любой — (любимый —
Ты). — Прискорбнейшее из событий.
— В Новостях и в Днях. — Статью дадите?
— Где? — В горах. (Окно в еловых ветках.
Простыня.) — Не видите газет ведь?
Так статью? — Нет. — Но . . . — Прошу избавить.
Вслух: трудна. Внутрь: не христопродавец.
— В санатории. (В раю наемном.)
— День? — Вчера, позавчера, не помню.
В Альказаре будете? — Не буду.
Вслух: семья. Внутрь: всё, но не Иуда.

С наступающим! (Рождался завтра!) —
Рассказать, что сделала, узнав про..?
Тсс . . . Оговорилась. По привычке.

Жизнь и смерть давно беру в кавычки,
Как заведомо-пустые сплёты.
Ничего не сделала, но что-то
Сделалось, без тени и без эха
Делающее!
Теперь — как ехал?
Как рвалось и не разорвалось как —
Сердце? Как на рысаках орловских,
От орлов, сказал, не отстающих,
Дух захватывало — или пуще?
Слаще? Ни высот тому, ни спусков,
На орлах летал заправских русских —
Кто. Связь кровная у нас с тем светом:
На Руси бывал — тот свет на этом
Зрел. Налаженная перебежка!
Жизнь и смерть произношу с усмешкой,
Скрытою — своей ее коснешься!
Жизнь и смерть произношу со сноской,
Звездочкою (ночь, которой чаю:
Вместо мозгового полушарья —
Звездное!)
Не позабыть бы, друг мой,
Следующего: что если буквы
Русские пошли взамен немецких —
То не потому, что нынче, дескать,
Всё сойдет, что мертвый (нищий) всё съест —
Не сморгнет! — а потому что тот свет,
Наш, — тринадцати, в Новодевичьем
Поняла: не без- а все-язычен.

Вот и спрашиваю не без грусти:
Уж не спрашиваешь, как по-русски
Nest?* Единственная, и все гнезда
Покрывающая рифма: звезды.

Отвлекаюсь? Но такой и вещи
Не найдется — от тебя отвлечься.
Каждый помысел, любой, Du Lieber**,
Слог в тебя ведет — о чем бы ни был
Толк (пусть русского родней немецкий
Мне, всех ангельский родней!) — как места
Несть, где нет тебя, нет есть: могила.
Всё как не было и всё как было,
— Неужели обо мне ничуть не? —
Окруженье, Райнер, самочувствье?
Настоятельно, всенепременно —
Первое видение вселенной
(Подразумевается, поэта
В оной) и последнее — планеты,
Раз только тебе и данной — в целом!
Не поэта с прахом, духа с телом,
(Обособить — оскорбить обоих)
А тебя с тобой, тебя с тобою ж,
— Быть Зевесовым не значит лучшим —
Кастора — тебя с тобой — Поллуксом,
Мрамора — тебя с тобою, травкой,
Не разлуку и не встречу — ставку
Очную: и встречу и разлуку
Первую.

На собственную руку

Как глядел (на след — на ней — чернильный)

Со своей столько-то (сколько?) мильной

Бесконечной ибо безначальной

Высоты над уровнем хрустальным

Средиземного — и прочих блюдец.

Всё как не было и всё как будет

И со мною за концом предместья.

Всё как не было и всё как есть уж

— Что списавшемуся до недельки

Лишней! — и куда ж еще глядеть-то,

Приоблокотясь на обод ложи,

С этого — как не на тот, с того же —

Как не на многострадальный этот.

В Беллевю живу. Из гнезд и веток

Городок. Переглянувшись с гидом:

Беллевю. Острог с прекрасным видом

На Париж — чертог химеры галльской —

На Париж — и на немножко дальше . . .

Приоблокотясь на алый обод,

Как тебе смешны (кому) «должно быть»,

(Мне ж) должны быть, с высоты без меры,

Наши Беллевю и Бельведеры!

Перебрасываюсь. Частность. Срочность.

Новый Год в дверях. За что, с кем чокнусь

Через стол? Чем? Вместо пены — ваты

Клок. Зачем? Ну, бьет — а при чем я тут?

Что мне делать в новогоднем шуме

С этой внутреннею рифмой: Райнер — умер.

Если ты, такое око смерклось,

Значит, жизнь не жизнь есть, смерть не смерть есть.

Значит — тмится, допойму при встрече! —

Нет ни жизни, нет ни смерти, — третье,

Новое. И за него (соломой

Застелив седьмой — двадцать шестому

Отходящему — какое счастье

Тобой кончиться, тобой начаться!)

Через стол, необозримый оком,

Буду чокаться с тобою тихим чоком

Стекла о стекло? Нет — не кабацким ихним:

Я о ты, слиясь дающих рифму:

Третье.

Через стол гляжу на крест твой.

Сколько мест — загородных, и места

Загородом! и кому же машет

Как не нам — куст? Мест — именно наших

И ничьих других! Весь лист! Вся хвоя!

Мест твоих со мной (твоих с тобою).

(Что с тобою бы и на массовку —

Говорить?) что — мест! а месяцов-то!

А недель! А дождевых предместий

Без людей! А утр! А всего вместе

И не начатого соловьями!

Верно, плохо вижу, ибо в яме,

Верно, лучше видишь, ибо свыше:

Ничего у нас с тобой не вышло.

До того, так чисто и так просто

Ничего, так по плечу и росту
Нам — что и перечислять не надо.
Ничего, кроме — не жди из ряду
Выходящего (неправ из такта
Выходящий!) — а в какой бы, как бы
Ряд вошедшего б?
Припев извечный:
Ничего хоть чем-нибудь на нечто
Что-нибудь — хоть издали бы — тень хоть
Тени! Ничего, что: час тот, день тот,
Дом тот — даже смертнику в колодках
Памятью дарованное: рот тот!

Или слишком разбирались в средствах?
Из всего того один лишь свет тот
Наш был, как мы сами только отсвет
Нас, — взамен всего сего — весь тот свет!

С незастроеннейшей из окраин —
С новым местом, Райнер, светом, Райнер!
С доказуемости мысом крайним —
С новым оком, Райнер, слухом, Райнер!

Всё тебе помехой
Было: страсть и друг.
С новым звуком, Эхо!
С новым эхом, Звук!

Сколько раз на школьном табурете:
Что за горы там? Какие реки?

Хороши ландшафты без туристов?
Не ошиблась, Райнер — рай — гористый,
Грозовой? Не притязаний вдовьих —
Не один ведь рай, над ним другой ведь
Рай? Террасами? Сужу по Татрам —
Рай не может не амфитеатром
Быть. (А занавес над кем-то спущен . . .)
Не ошиблась, Райнер, Бог — растущий
Баобаб? Не Золотой Людовик —
Не один ведь Бог? Над ним другой ведь
Бог?

Как пишется на новом месте?
Впрочем есть ты — есть стих: сам и есть ты —
Стих! Как пишется в хорошей жисти
Без стола для локтя, лба для кисти
(Горсти)?
— Весточку, привычным шифром!
Райнер, радуешься новым рифмам?
Ибо правильно толкуя слово
Рифма — что — как не — целый ряд новых
Рифм — Смерть?
Некуда: язык изучен.
Целый ряд значений и созвучий
Новых.
— До свиданья! До знакомства!
Свидимся — не знаю, но — споемся.
С мне-самой неведомой землею —
С целым морем, Райнер, с целой мною!

Не разъехаться — черкни заране.
С новым звуконачертаньем, Райнер!

В небе лестница, по ней с Дарами . . .
С новым рукоположеньем, Райнер!

— Чтоб не залили, держу ладонью. —
Поверх Роны и поверх Rarogn'a
Поверх явной и сплошной разлуки
Райнеру — Мариа — Рильке — в руки.

Bellevue, 7 февраля 1927

Biographical Note
For The Translator

Mary Jane White is a poet and translator who practiced law at
her home, the O. J. Hager House in Waukon, Iowa. She was
born and raised in North Carolina, earned degrees from The
North Carolina School of the Arts, Reed College, The University
of Iowa Writers' Workshop, and studied law at Duke University,
graduating from The University of Iowa. Her poetry and translations received NEA Fellowships in 1979 and 1985. She taught
lyric poetry and poetry workshops briefly at the University of
Iowa and at Luther College in Decorah, Iowa, and served for a

decade as an Iowa Poet in the Schools, before her son, Ruffin, was born in 1991. She has been awarded writing scholarships to Bread Loaf (1979), Squaw Valley Community of Writers (2006), Bread Loaf Translators' Conference (2015), Writers in Paradise Conference (2016), Prague Summer Program for Writers (2017) Summer Literary Seminars in Tbilisi, Georgia (2018). Her first book *Starry Sky to Starry Sky* (1988) is still available from Holy Cow! Press, and contains translations of Marina Tsvetaeva's long, lyric cycle, "Miles," which first appeared as an inserted feature in *The American Poetry Review.* Earlier poems and other translations including translations of Eugenio Montale from Italian have appeared in *Adelaide, AGNI* (online), *The Anthology of Magazine Verse and Yearbook of American Poetry, The American Poetry Review, Appalachian Heritage, Archaeopteryx: The Newman Journal of Ideas, The Black Warrior Review, Crazyhorse, Cutthroat, E-Ratio, The Iowa Review, The Louisville Review, Luna Tack, The Peacock Review, Nimrod, International Journal of Poetry and Prose, New Directions 46: An International Anthology of Poetry and Prose, Rockhurst Review, Two Cities Review, Verse-Virtual, Water Table, Willow Springs, The Winter Anthology, Writers' Forum 7,* have been featured on Iowa Public Radio, and included in various anthologies: *Russian Poetry: The Modern Period* (University of Iowa Press, 1978), ed. by Daniel Weissbort and John Glad, a New York Times Notable Book of the Year; *Voices on the Landscape: Contemporary Iowa Poets* (Loess Hills Books, 1996); and *Discoveries, New Writing from The Iowa Review,* (Iowa City: University of Iowa Press, 2012). Portions of "Girlfriend," Marina Tsvetaeva's cycle of love poems for the Russian poet Sophia Parnok have appeared in *Epicenter* and *Drunken Boat.*

Made in the USA
Middletown, DE
07 May 2022

65450960R00326